# Herbartianism and its Educational Consequences in the Period of the Austro-Hungarian Monarchy

ERZIEHUNG IN WISSENSCHAFT UND PRAXIS

Herausgegeben von Johanna Hopfner

BAND 10

PETER LANG
EDITION

Edvard Protner

# Herbartianism and its Educational Consequences in the Period of the Austro-Hungarian Monarchy

## The Case of Slovenia

PETER LANG
EDITION

**Bibliographic Information published by the Deutsche Nationalbibliothek**
The Deutsche Nationalbibliothek lists this publication in the Deutsche Nationalbibliografie; detailed bibliographic data is available in the internet at http://dnb.d-nb.de.

Printed with financial support of the Slovenian Research Agency, the Province of Styra, the Austrian Cultural Forum Ljubljana and the Faculty of Regional and Educational Sciences University of Graz.

Peer reviewed by Prof. Dr. Mojca Peček Čuk and Prof. Dr. Majda Cencič

**Library of Congress Cataloging-in-Publication Data**
Protner, Edvard.
Herbartianism and its educational consequences in the period of the Austro-Hungarian monarchy : the case of Slovenia / Edvard Protner.
pages cm. -- (Erziehung in Wissenschaft und Praxis)
ISBN 978-3-631-64881-0
1. Herbart, Johann Friedrich, 1776-1841--Influence. 2. Education--Slovenia--History. 3. Teachers--Training of--Slovenia--History. I. Title.
LB648.P74 2014
370.1--dc23

2014018785

ISSN 1861-9770
ISBN 978-3-631-64881-0 (Print)
E-ISBN 978-3-653-03911-5 (E-Book)
DOI 10.3726/ 978-3-653-03911-5


Peter Lang Edition is an Imprint of Peter Lang GmbH.
Peter Lang – Frankfurt am Main · Bern · Bruxelles · New York · Oxford · Warszawa · Wien


This publication has been peer reviewed.
www.peterlang.com

To Jaša

# Contents

# Introduction

## I.

The term "Herbartianism" is foreign to most people. We can assume that it is also relatively unknown among those involved in the pedagogical sciences. The term is associated with the pedagogic doctrine developed in the first half of the nineteenth century by Johann Friedrich Herbart and established in the second half of the nineteenth century by his followers. Let us look what kind of definition can be found by those who would like to learn about the concept with the help of the Internet. The first result various search engines usually give is from the *Encyclopaedia Britannica*, which states: "**Herbartianism**, pedagogical system of German educator Johann Friedrich Herbart (1776–1841). Herbart's educational ideas, which applied particularly to the instruction of adolescents, had a profound influence on late 19th-century teaching practices, especially in the United States, where educators established the National Herbart Society in 1895. Herbart advocated five formal steps in teaching: (1) preparation—a process of relating new material to be learned to relevant past ideas or memories in order to give the pupil a vital interest in the topic under consideration; (2) presentation—presenting new material by means of concrete objects or actual experience; (3) association—thorough assimilation of the new idea through comparison with former ideas and consideration of their similarities and differences in order to implant the new idea in the mind; (4) generalization—a procedure especially important to the instruction of adolescents and designed to develop the mind beyond the level of perception and the concrete; (5) application—using acquired knowledge not in a purely utilitarian way but so that every learned idea becomes a part of the functional mind and an aid to a clear, vital interpretation of life. This step is presumed possible only if the student immediately applies the new idea, making it his own. Enthusiasm for Herbartianism declined with the appearance of new pedagogical theories, in particular those of John Dewey" ("Herbartianism", s.d.).

While this definition presents some of the key points of Herbartianism, it also distorts the concept by giving misleading and even incorrect information. The concept of Herbartianism is undoubtedly linked to Johann Friedrich Herbart and his pedagogic ideas, which influenced teaching practises in the second half of the nineteenth century. Nevertheless, we must to take into account that this practise was not influenced by Herbart's ideas directly, but indirectly, through the teachings developed by the followers of Herbart's pedagogic ideas. It is also true that teachers in the United States founded the National Herbart Society in 1895. But the statement that these ideas had a "profound influence… especially in the United States" is misleading. These ideas had a far greater influence in European countries, especially German-speaking ones, as well as in countries which were under strong German influence, such as all countries that were part of the Hapsburg Monarchy and later, the Austro-Hungarian Monarchy. In Europe, the substantial impact of Herbartianism can also be seen in France, England, and the Scandinavian countries, but also in South America and Japan.

Other statements in this short definition are also similary misleading or even false. It is not true that his ideas were applied particularly to the education of adolescents. In the second half of the nineteenth century, these ideas were much more present in elementary and primary education than in secondary education, which encompasses adolescents.

Furthermore, the statement that Herbart advocated "five formal steps in teaching" is completely false. Herbart actually defined four steps of class articulation, in connection with the psychological laws of learning and teaching: Clarity, Association, System, Method. The five above-mentioned formal steps originated with Wilhelm Rein (cf. Dunkel 1970, 230), one of the leading Herbaritanists, i.e. the followers of Herbart's ideas[1]. But this false claim is symptomatic for the reception of Herbartianism within broader circles of experts in two ways. First, it points to an unjustifiable reduction of the wealth of theoretical concepts created by Herbart and the Herbartians down to the mere didactic articulation of classes. Second, the implicit message of this point simply equates Herbart's ideas with the ideas of Herbartians, which is even more problematic.

It is true that "enthusiasm for Herbartianism declined with the appearance of new pedagogical theories," but the reduction to Dewy's theory raises further problems because Herbartianism limits the concept, unjustifiably, to the United States. One key fact is overlooked: European textbooks on educational history and pedagogics describe, almost without exception, how the reformist pedagogic movement at the turn of the century was battling a Herbartianist pedagogic paradigm.

On Internet pages in English we can find more accurate definitions of the concept of Herbartianism, but one would soon notice the imbalance between the meaning

1 The genesis of the theory of formal steps in classes from Herbart's conceptualisation to the conceptualisation of Herbartians is thoroughly analysed by Scheffler (1977).

attributed to Herbartianism and its influence on school practises in the second half of the nineteenth century, as well as the research attention which has been devoted to this topic in the Anglo-Saxon as well as European region. There are already issues at the level of designation. Searching for the concept 'Herbartianism' on the web often gives back results with the term 'Herbartism'. Which term is more suitable? I choose to follow the term used in current research as a criterion of suitability. It is a fact that 'Herbartianism' appears in the titles of works authored by contemporaries in the movement, e.g. F. H. Hayward and F. E. Thomas' *The Critics of Herbartianism and other matter* [sic] *contributory to the study of the Herbartian question (1903)*; H. B. Dunkel's *Herbart and Herbartianism: An Educational Ghost Story* (1970), a standard text in the field; and K. Cruikshank's more recent doctoral dissertation *The Rise and Fall of American Herbartianism: Dynamics of an Educational Reform Movement* (1993) show that the term Herbartianism is well established and widely used by experts.

But nonetheless, why do we not use Herbartism instead of Herbartianism if we observe the analogy with, for instance, that Marx gave rise to Marxism, and not Marxianism? The purpose of this discussion is not an etymological explanation of this term, but to define the terms of this study. It is important to point out that a similar dilemma also appeared in German pedagogic terminology. German speakers also generally use the established term 'Herbartianismus' along with 'Herbartismus'. In the introduction to the edited collection *Herbartianist Pedagogy in the Austrian-Hungarian Monarchy* (2009), an interesting editorial explanation is given by E. Adam and G. Grimm: "To avoid terminological misunderstandings, we use 'Herbartian' [Herbartianisch] when we mean Herbart's pedagogy and 'Herbartianistic' [Herbartianistisch] when we mean Herbartians"[2] (4). Thus, it would be more than reasonable to distinguish between the term, 'Herbartism' which would mean Herbart's pedagogic theory and 'Herbartianism', which would reference the study of the pedagogic ideas developed by Herbart's followers. The terminological distinction made by Adam and Grimm is important, but it does not seem that it is widely known, acknowledged or established. The reasons for this can be attributed to the fact that Herbartianism is an under-researched topic and that the distinction between the pedagogic theories of Herbart and the Herbartians has not yet been firmly established. To avoid any potential misunderstandings, we will use the term Herbartianism to refer to the pedagogic ideas of Herbartians, and not to Herbart's pedagogic ideas themselves.

2 All quotes in this book which are in original German or Slovenian were translated into English by Vid Hudrap.

In Slovenia, this terminological dilemma is not an issue because we only use the term 'herbartizem', which is analogous to the English term 'Herbartism' and the German term 'Herbartismus'. The Slovene *Multilingual Terminological Dictionary of Education* defines Herbartianism as follows: "Herbartism is a curricular movement of the late 19th century led by the followers of the German philosopher Johann Friedrich Herbart, commonly known as the father of scientific teaching in education. The movement supported a liberal-humanistic curriculum which was founded on history and literature. Teaching and learning was divided into five stages: preparation, presentation, association, generalization, application. The theoretical basis of this curriculum was the idea that education is connecting previously gathered experiences with new ones" (Herbartizem, s.d.).

This definition is acceptable, although saying that the movement supported a liberal-humanistic curriculum is too categorical and cannot be generalised to all followers of this doctrine. Although it is interesting to find look at the analogue terms in English and German, this effort is not very helpful for the Slovene research community, who would like to find a suitable synonym for the term 'herbartizem' in English or German. In this dictionary, the Slovene term "herbartizem" gives the English "herbartian movement" and the German, "Herbartismus". None of the terms offered are completely incorrect, but they are also not precise enough. We can conclude, however, that Herbartianism is the established term within the English and Anglo-Saxon pedagogic tradition, and in the German-speaking world, "Herbartianismus" is preferred.

## II.

The above-mentioned terminological dilemmas suggest (as we have argued above) that research on this doctrine has remained at the edge of interest in pedagogic historiography. When I decided to make the problem of the concept of Herbartianism in the education of teachers in Slovenia the topic of my doctoral dissertation, I knew then that my understanding of Herbartianism, which I gained during my previous pedagogical studies, was incomplete, but I could not imagine that I was so misinformed. Herbartianism was taught to students in a characteristicly negative evaluative context, which is also present in textbooks on the history of European pedagogy throughout the continent. It is a critique that accuses Herbartianist pedagogy of schematism, formalism, mechanicism, and intellectualism, among other "-isms". I remember our professor illustrating the weaknesses of Herbartianist pedagogy with an anecdote: When Herbartianist theory was dominant in the educational system, school inspectors would regularly enter classrooms and demand that the teacher explain which formal step they were currently at in the lesson. This anecdote presents the typical stereotype of Herbartianism, which was internalised by generations of students. But this approach did not establish only itself among those with Bachelor degrees in Pedagogy, but also in the numerous generations of teachers working at various educational levels in the postwar era (cf. Protner 2009). Vlado Schmidt, one of the leading authorities on Slovene pedagogy, wrote in 1949: "Herbartianist scheme is a frozen, rigid regulation which wants to be valid 'always and everywhere and because of this it is valid no time and no place'. This is a typical love of a German philistine to a systematics settled once and for all which had at one time been fatally established also in our pedagogy and it is still our job to root it out. This formalism has led so far that the school supervisors once evaluated the class mostly on the basis of its formal structure" (Schmidt 1949, 219). This is a stereotype that could not be avoided by almost any teacher in postwar Slovenia because Schmit's books were a compulsory part of the curriculum until the 1970s and 1980s.

I can also remember that the anecdote about the rigidity of Herbartianism was supplemented by the information that this triggered a resistance of teachers and that the teachers were supported in this by Viktor Bežek, at that time the teacher and later headmaster of the teacher training college. Bežek had a long dispute with the territorial school inspector and advocate of Herbartianist doctrine, Fran Hubad, and stood for a more modern didactic concept (more about this polemic in Chapter 3). The myth of the rigidity of Herbartianism was joined here by the myth of the role of Viktor Bežek in this dispute, which was transmitted from generation to generation in the Slovene pedagogic historiography and was used to fortify the negative evaluative image of Herbartianism. The myth was further entrenched by the suggestion that resistance to Herbartianism automatically means the promotion of progress. Whoever henceforth was an opponent of Herbartianism could thus be recognised a progressive pedagogue worthy of praise.

This view on Herbartianism holds some truth. Browsing through the sources (which will be presented in detail in Chapter 3) shows that the anecdote about the school supervisor is true and that the description of formalism of the didactic image of school practise is real. Indeed, the polemic described started in 1903 with the critique of such practises by one of the primary school inspectors in Ljubljana.

Leading Slovene pedagogues found this anecdote half a century later cited in Bežek's text and used it for the following half century when illustrating and interpreting Herbartianism. Due to the lack of more serious analysis of Herbartianism, this banal example gave a firm footing to the stereotype: Herbart is equal to Herbartianism, which are equal to formal steps and didactic template. In short: "old school".

The belief that Herbart cannot be neatly equated with Herbartianism has long been known to authors working in this field. This may seem paradoxical, but we can say that the first steps towards Herbart's rehabilitation had already been made by Herbartians themselves. Herbartianist pedagogy was never a monolith pedagogic theory: Different currents within Herbartianism had strong disagreements from the start, and these were rooted in differing attitudes towards Herbart and obligations towards his theory. The generally established pattern of interpretation, which many representatives of reformist pedagogy criticised as schematism, formalism and dogmaticism of Herbartianism, fails to see with which force these weaknesses were criticised by some of the typical Herbartians (Fröhlich 1883/1901). The most notable was the disagreement between Karl Volkmar Stoy and the prevailing thought Tuiscon Ziller. A characteristic representative of the opposition within Herbartianism, whose pedagogic concept largely relied on Stoy's pedagogy, evaluated Ziller's teachings on the formal steps as follows: "The effort to perscribe everything into the smallest detail, argue and derive from general principles has led to a petty school craft pedantry, to dead and suffocating schematism, to utterly unnatural artificiality, to almighty dialectic artifices and shiny virtual basis…general truths are challenged and refuted, the thoughts, right in their own sense, are twisted with exaggeration, proven didactic rules are made infeasible with pedantic rules" (Richter 1887/1908, 177).

The critics from the circle of reformist pedagogy really did not have it hard when it came to criticising the so-called *old school*—even in the critique of the formal steps, the terminological pattern of the description could be found by the Herbartians themselves. In Richter's clash with Ziller's school of thought, his efforts to shield Herbart from the critique is worth close attention. Herbartianism's strategy of defence against the critique, with which many Herbartians also identified themselves, was based on the return to the original Herbart, as it was Richter's opinion, that "[t]here came to a situation in Ziller's school that with the adjective 'Herbart+Ziller', which became common, was meant as a violation against Herbart and was attributed that which belonged only to Ziller and against which Herbart would strongly protest" (Ibid., 200). References to Herbart and his interpretation were utilised on the one hand as a critique of some Herbartianist derivations, and on the other hand, as defence against criticism from other pedagogic fields. This argument held that Herbar's pedagogic theory was far more compatible with modern pedagogic efforts than as a theory of that dominant (Ziller's) school of thought within Herbartianism, which was presented to the public as the only true "scientific pedagogy".

A characteristic example of such argumentation is Dietering's 1908 book *Herbart's Pedagogy from the Standpoint of Modern Educational Efforts*. Similarly to Richter, he also points out that some Herbartians interpreted "the master's ideas" very arbitrarily and turned them into a rigid system that does not have much in common with that of Herbart. Dietering identifies the emphasised role of teacher personality as the leading trend in modern pedagogy; within this framework he had to deal with the accusation that Herbartianism gave priority to the method of the teacher. His defence against this accusation was based on proving that Herbart's pedagogy was indeed closer to personality pedagogy than the rigid formalism and dogmatism of Ziller's teachings within Herbartianism. This was supported with the claim that even E. Linde, the founder of personality pedagogy, found a strong intuitive-personality component in Herbart's pedagogy and was very enthusiastic about it (Dietering 1908, 5). Herbartianist pedagogy found itself before its biggest challenge when it finally had to articulate the relationship between teacher personality and its influence on the pedagogic process, as opposed to the role of methods. This was discussed in 1912 in the Society for Scientific Pedagogy[3]. Linde personally attended this general assembly although he was not a member of the Society. His understanding of personality was exposed to sharp criticism and the unifying of opinions that resulted was not to anyone's satisfaction (Maier 1940, 126). The fact that the dialogue was even opened shows that there were certain changes occuring within Herbartianism. In addition to this, personality pedagogy and Herbartianism already had a common enemy at that time: The child-focused reformist pedagogy movement. Linde and Herbartians had an equally negative opinion about, for instance, L. Gurlitt and Ellen Key. Thus, the yearly report for 1913 featured Linde's opinion that "we, the elder, the true personality pedagogues, acknowledge objective pedagogic norms which are irrefutably valid but must not be used mechanically. Newer personality pedagogues reject all objective norms and do not know another law then their own individual nature" (Ibid., 127).

At the end of Herbartianist dominance, we thus find the last desperate attempts to legitimise the theory by proving that Herbart's theory was misused; this was connected with the appeal to read Herbart differently. But during the time between both wars, the dominance of other pedagogic concepts was so strong that this

3 In original: *Verein für wissenschaftliche Pädagogik*. The Society was formed in 1868 in Leipzig, Germany and represents the central authority responsible for the systematic spreading of Herbartianist doctrine. The first president of the society was T. Ziller. The organisational characteristics and the characteristics of the content of this Society have been thoroughly described by Maier (1940).

appeal could not have succeeded. A look at the secondary literature on Herbart reveals that the interest in researching Herbart is also present between both wars, but it was only during the first years after the war when interpretations were brought about that would justify using the term "Herbart Renaissance" (Koschnitzke 1988). Renewed interest in Herbart was generated mainly by Herman Nohl (1948) and Walter Asmus (1948, 1950/51); and we take it somewhat for granted that this happened in the scope of arts pedagogy[4]. Here we can look for continuity with those Herbartians (e.g. the aforementioned Dietering) who believed that the significance of a teacher's personality was emphasised more in Herbart's pedagogy than teacher's didactic method. A pattern of interpretation continued, which asserted that the weaknesses of Herbartianist pedagogy were not to be blamed on Herbart, and the more Herbart was praised, the more a negative view of Herbartianist pedagogy, i.e. the pedagogy of Herbart's followers, took hold. Typical examples of this pattern are seen in Bernhard Schwenk's *Understanding Herbart and Herbartians* (1963), Harold B. Dunkel's *Herbart and Herbartianism* (1970), and in Bruno M. Bellerate *J.F. Herbart and the Justification of Scientific Pedagogy in Germany* (1979). All three titles promise a discussion on Herbartianism but do not deliver an analysis of the Herbartianism. Instead, all three works mostly analyse Herbart's pedagogy; only a tenth of the text is devoted to Herbartianism. Of course, this degree of research attention could not shift the mainstream stereotype of Herbartianism, but this is also not the purpose of these texts.

The role of key individual representatives of Herbartianism was long determined in the historical memory of the expert community by the fact that the researchers of this doctrine were mostly satisfied with generally established stereotypical presentations, which were not based on deep analyses of the original texts (as was the case for a long time with Herbart). Greater shifts in Herbartianism's reception started happening only after these authors became subject to more detailed analysis. A review of three such monographs shows an interesting similarity. The monograph about Wilhelm Rein is concluded by Horst-Erich Pohl (1972) with the chapter titled "Rein–A Herbartian?"(Ibid., 275ff), which argues that Rein cannot be equated with Ziller. A similar monograph about Karl Volkmar Stoy is concluded by Rotraud Coriand, with a chapter titled "Karl Volkmar Stoy - a Herbartian?" (2000), which also asserts that Stoy cannot be compared to Ziller. Finally, it is important to mention Heribart Scheffler's monograph, *Ziller's theory on formal steps and the accusation about teaching methodology schematism*

4 In the German pedagogic tradition, this pedagogic concept is known as "Geisteswissenschaftliche Pädagogik".

(1970). Although Scheffler does not explicitly pose the question of whether Ziller was a Herbartian, the basic findings of his monograph state that "the judgement of Ziller's theory of formal steps, which was very firmly formulated by the movement for working school and was sharpened by the Herbart renaissance, is not true" and that "Ziller's step theory was conceived much less schematically and mechanicistically as it was perceived by the following generations[.]" (Ibid., 8). We could read this ironically—that even Ziller cannot be equated with Ziller—and ask ourselves: Was Tuiscon Ziller a Herbartian? In any case, this example also shows that a thorough investigation of Ziller's pedagogic theory shows a fundamentally different picture than the pedagogic historiography would suggest.

With the recent renewed interest in Herbartianism, its traditional reception fundamentally changed. The critique of the generally negative cliché of Herbartianism is coming to the fore as an independent research issue, especially in relation to the formal steps. Oelkers, who calls this cliché the "standard of condemnation" (1998, 132), pointed to individual elements of the formation of *negativimages* as early as 1989 when he analysed the decline of Herbartianist pedagogy (Oelkers 1989); he discussed this more into detail a decade later, when he wrote: "The pejorative expression 'Herbartianism' is necessary to even have something like 'reformist pedagogy' effectively delimited and exposed. The expression does not describe any historical reality, neither in the theoretical, nor in the practical sense. Clichés are debated which are formulated with a polemic purpose to withdraw from their initial context and then become historically independent. The pedagogic reflection which followed took over these clichés and lexicographically fixed them" (Oelkers 1998, 131).

# III.

It seems that the interest in researching Herbartianism in German-speaking regions has increased in the last two decades. The monograph by Peter Metz *Herbartianism as Paradigm for Profesionalization and School Reform* (1992) can be considered a standard work from this field. It investigates the effects of Herbartianism in Switzerland, but also gives a fundamental outline of the theoretical and organisational dimensions of Herbartianism, along with an objective study of Tuiskon Ziller as a key actor in this movement. His work is complemented by Rotraud Coriand's published habilitation, *Karl Volkmar Stoy and the Idea of Pedagogical Education* (2000), which enables greater insight into the differences between the two key actors within Herbartianist pedagogy. Coriand has had a long-standing interest in

Herbartianism; at the end of the 1990s, she established a centre for researching Herbartianism [Hebrtianismus Forschungstelle] at the Friedrich Schiller University in Jena, Germany. This research initiative moved with her to her subsequent position at University of Duisgurg-Essen under the name "Working Group for International Herbartianism Research" [Arbeitsstelle für Internationale Herbartianismusforschung]. The Working Group's web page describes two objectives. Firstly, it lists research projects in the field. Secondly, it works to facilitate international exchange of research on Herbartianism. An international work group was also established for this purpose on the 22 November 1997. The team's efforts helped connect researchers of Herbartianism from different national backgrounds, namely at two conferences and two published collections: *Herbartianism–A Forgotten Scientific Story* (Coriand and Winkler 1998) and *The Herbartianist Concept of Training Teachers: History or Challenge*? (Coriand 2003). Coriand gathered a wide circle of contributors for both collections, which shed light on the character of Herbartianism around the world, from the United States, to European countries and Japan. Along with important studies in German language, which apart from analysing Herbart's views also touch on the issue of Herbartianist pedagogy (e.g. Schwenk 1963, Jacobs 1993) and the articles that analyse more prominent individual Herbartians (some of which were covered in the previous section)[5], the understanding of Herbartianism in recent years was also enriched by B. Dollinger et al.'s *Social Pedagogy and Herbartianism* (2010), which analyses the contribution of Herbartianism to social pedagogy.

A completely new dimension of research on Herbartianism was enabled by Rotraud Coriand by establishing a webpage[6], which offers the interested scientific community two exceptionally comprehensive and useful data banks:

1) The personal data base covers approximately 7,000 publication titles by the approximately seven hundred authors who form the historical 'Herbartianist circle' (as of 16 August 2010) in the period between 1809 and 1938. Approximately 5,700 titles by about five hundred authors are connected to this narrow pedagogic field

5 Here it is also important to mention the doctoral thesis of Emile Müller (2000) which analyses and compares pedagogic ideas and institutional derivations of four key Herbartians: Stoy, Ziller, Dörpfeld and Rein.

6 It is a result of the research project under the leadership of Rotraud Coriand titled *Bio-doxographic corpus of pedagogical Herbartianismus* [*Bio-doxographisches Korpus Pädagogischer Herbartianismus*], financed by the German Research Association [Deutsche Forschungsgemeinschaft] (cf. Abgeschlossene Projekte, s.d.). A more detailed description of the project can be found in Coriand, Böhme, and Henkel (2003).

(Coriand, Grundig de Vazquez, Henkel and Böhme 2011; c.f. Coriand 2010, 9; Coriand 2010a, 9).
2) The newspaper database covers almost 10,000 titles in 20 journals edited by Herbartians during the period between 1838 and 1936. Articles of non-Herbartians are also covered (Coriand, Henkel 2013; c.f. Coriand, 2010, 9; Coriand 2010a, 9).

Both bibliographies provide biographies of 36 of the most characteristic representatives of Herbartianist pedagogy, which can be found on the same web page (Coriand, Henkel and Böhme 2013). The sheer number of sources evinces the comprehensiveness of research on Herbartianism. This impression is rounded out by the systematisation of Herbartianist literature along pedagogic subject fields (Coriand 2010, Coriand 2010a) which finally refutes the unjustified reduction of Herbartianist pedagogic theory to formal steps because it offers an insight (with its volume) into the wide diversity of pedagogically relevant topics and fields Herbartians dealt with.

An increase in interest for Herbartianism can also be seen in those European countries where traditionally German pedagogic thought was strongly present. One of the few monographs (along with Metz) that comprehensively analyses the presence of Herbartianism in a certain national environments and is accessible to the general scientific community in the German language, is the Oleg Zajakin's 2004 monograph titled *The Reception of Herbartianism in Russian Pedagogy since the Middle of the 19th Century*, which demonstrates how Herbartianist pedagogy was present in Russia even before other regions of Europe. His interpretations of the ideological backgrounds which influenced the reception of Herbartianist pedagogical ideas and ideas of Herbartians in the Soviet Union are particularly interesting. It is possible to assume that there are other important academic analyses of Herbartianism in other languages[7], but these studies remain less accessible to the wider scientific community than those published in German or English.

Today, because English is the lingua franca of international scientific discourse, texts written in English are accessible to the broadest circle of researchers. But the scope of secondary (and of course particularly primary) sources connected with Herbartianism in English compared to German still remains modest. Research in English mainly deals with the presence of Herbartianism in the United States

7 Interest for Herbartianism is also present in Italy (e.g. Volpicelli 2003). Nataša Vujisić Živkovič examines the presence of Herbartianism in Serbia by analysing the work of one of the leading Serbian pedagogues of the nineteenth century (2012).

and England, and far less in continental Europe. Among modern studies of note, in addition to the aforementioned monograph of Harold B. Dunkel *Herbart and Herbartianism: An Educational Ghost Story* (1970), there is also a series of PhD theses[8] that show a lively interest in this field of American history of pedagogic thought. These works, however, are mostly inaccessible to the wider circle of researchers in other parts of the world. Studies of contemporaries who analyse Herbartianism as a pedagogic phenomenon of its time (e.g. De Garmo 1895; Dodd 1898, 2010; Darroch 1903; Felkin and Felkin 1900; Hayward 1904; Mc Murry 1903; Randels 1909; see also the translation of Ufer 1894) are still very relevant to Herbartianism research in the United States and England. The bibliographies in the above-mentioned monographs show a relatively rich reception of this pedagogic concept at the turn of the century. Hayward's concrete demonstration (1903) of the ideas of Herbart and key Herbartians stands out as an especially valuable systematic display of critics of Herbartianist pedagogy. This work also features an annotated list of Herbartianist literature in English (see also Dunkel 1970) and confirms the presence of Herbartianism in Germany, Britain, America and elsewhere around the world.

At the end of the 1990s, I was writing my doctoral dissertation on Herbartianism[9] independently but almost at the same time as Rotraud Coriand and Kathleen Cruikshank were conducting their research on the subject.[10] In the following years, the topic remained a regular feature of my research work. The jubilee anniversary of one of Henrik Schreiner, a prominent Slovene Herbartian, made me think

8 See, for example (cf. American Herbartians, s. d.):
Cruikshank, Kathleen Anne. *The Rise And Fall Of American Herbartianism: Dynamics Of An Educational Reform Movement*. Ph.D. Dissertation: The University of Wisconsin. Madison: 1993,
Winters, Marilyn B. *The Course Of Study In American Education: Past, Present And Future*. Ph.D. Dissertation: The Claremont Graduate University. Claremont, CA: 1984.
Tyler, Kenneth Dean. *The Educational Life And Work Of Charles A. McMurry: 1872-1929*. Ed.D Dissertation: Northern Illinois University. DeKalb: 1982.
Hendon, Ursula Stendel. *Herbart's Concept Of Morality In Education And Its Role In America*. Ph.D. Dissertation: The University of Alabama. Tuscaloosa: 1980.
Westfall, Barry Howard. *German Educational Thought Adapted To American Schools: Herbartian Influence On American Teacher Education Through Selected Publications Of Charles De Garmo, And Charles And Frank McMurry*. Ed.D. Dissertation: Northern Illinois University. Dekalb: 1975.

9 A modified doctoral thesis was published under the title *Herbartianist Pedagogy in Slovenia* (1869–1914) (Protner 2001).

10 My conclusions on her dissertation are based on referrences in Cruikshank (1998).

that it would be interesting to better understand the presence of Herbartianism in neighbouring countries. We organised a symposium in 2001 in celebration of Schreiner's jubilee (Protner 2002), which was attended by colleagues from neighbouring Austria (Adam 2002), Croatia (Radeka 2002, Dumbović 2002) and Hungary (Brezsnyánszky 2002). The international participation was not extensive but it generated an initiative to approach the presence of Herbartianism in the field of the Austro-Hungarian Monarchy more systematically (cf. Adam and Grimm 2009, 6). In 2006, Adam and Grimm organised a meeting of researchers from Austria, Germany, Slovenia, Hungary, Croatia and Bulgaria at the University of Klagenfurt, Austria. The result of this meeting was a collection of scientific papers titled *Herbartianist Pedagogy in the Austrian-Hungarian Monarchy* (Adam and Grimm 2009). It is an important contribution to the understanding of school doctrine in the context of the national unit, which was the second largest European country after Russia before the First World War. Before its breakup, the borders of the Monarchy stretched on the territory, which is today comprised of Austria, the Czech Republic, Slovakia, Italy, Slovenia, Croatia, Bosnia and Herzegovina, Hungary, Romania, Poland and Ukraine. In all these countries, the national history of school and pedagogy is closely related to the Hapsburg and later Austro-Hungarian school legislation and pedagogic currents that came from the German-speaking regions. The research of national history in the aforementioned countries thus overlaps greatly with the Austrian history of schooling and pedagogy. Thus, the basic work of the Austrian school historiography are for instance Engelbrecht's *History of the Austrian School System* (1986), or Gönner's monograph *Austrian Education of Teachers from Normal School to Pedagogic Academy* (1967). It is important to point to the comprehensive study of W. Brezinka (2000, 2003, 2008) titled *Pedagogy in Austria*, in which the author analyses the presence of pedagogy as a university discipline at those universities of the Austro-Hungarian Monarchy located in present-day Austria[11]. His analysis covers the time from the Age of Enlightenment onwards, when first departments of pedagogy started emerging at Austrian universities, to the present. Within this scope, Brezinka also analyses pedagogic ideas and the academic contribution of some of the key representatives of Herbartianism (i.e. G. A. Lindner, O. Willman, T. Vogt), who helped shape this pedagogic field not only in Austria, but also in Germany (where Herbartianism originated)

11 The fourth part is forthcoming, in which the author analyses the presence of pedagogy at the Vienna Economic University [Wirtschaftsuniversität Vienna] and the University in Klagenfurt, Austria. It also features an overview and balance (correspondence with author).

and elsewhere. This had a particular effect in Slovenia, which got its own national university in 1919 after the breakup of the Austro-Hungarian Monarchy.

It is impossible to thoroughly sum up the state of research on Herbartianism in this short introductory chapter. But this summary again confirms that in comparison to the institutional, scientific and practical school influence that Herbartianism had, this pedagogic doctrine is still underexplored.

## IV.

Researching Herbartianism is very difficult without proficiency in German. The monographs published in English on this topic are of good quality; they offer solid, basic information and enable an understanding of the influence and presence of Herbartianism (mostly) in England and the United States. Nevertheless, English literature in this field is not rich enough to enable a thorough understanding of all the facets of Herbartianism covered in the last two decades by studies in German. Above all, though, the existing literature is not rich enough to enable insight into the influence of Herbartianism on the image of the school in the scope of the Austro-Hungarian Monarchy, the territory frequently equated with Central Europe. The situation in Slovenia cannot be unambiguously generalised for the whole territory of Austria-Hungary, but it is representative enough to help the reader form an impression of the school in an environment where the whole bureaucratic legislative framework also followed the pedagogic doctrine. This English-language monograph tries to bridge the language barriers that arise when researching this topic and thus contributes to the knowledge of the genesis and presence of one of the central pedagogic concepts of modern school.

This book offers the translation of six articles originally published in Slovene, Italian and German in the last decade. Its ambition is not a comprehensive or systematic presentation of Herbartianist pedagogy. Every article presented a whole when it was created and each covers a certain section of the whole theme, but they can also be connected with a certain logic starting with Herbart's ideals and ending with their implementation in school practise at a typical provincial school.

The first chapter analyses and presents the pedagogic seminar Herbart set up in Königsberg during the first decade of the nineteenth century. This analysis uncovers some of the lesser-known views of Herbart. Here we see him as a representative of the opposition to Prussian school reform, which strived for greater enforcement of the power and influence of the state in education. Some ideas developed by Herbart are still relevant today. His position in opposition to State control of education in particular shows how far his concept is from that which was discussed by the Herbartians half a century later.

Some of Herbart's pedagogic ideas that contain theoretical relevance today are presented in the next chapter, which shows the theoretical background along with the methods and attempts used to construct a concept of teacher education in the scope of the third Austrian Primary School Act from 1869. This is the single most decisive law that defined the modern image of the school system in the entire Austro-Hungarian Monarchy, and thus, also in Slovenia. The main thesis of this chapter is that Herbartianism fundamentally contributed to the professionalism of the teaching profession at the turn of the century.

In the next chapter, we switch to the analysis of Herbartianism in the territory of Slovenia. The thesis of this chapter is that Herbartianism was present here even before it was theoretically articulated. When it became the subject of theoretical reflection, this happened at the same time a critical distance was developing towards Herbartianism. This chapter also analyses the difference in Herbartianism between different Slovene regions and demonstrates that it was more influenced by school bureaucracy than theoretical flows.

Research on Herbartianism is mostly directed towards the analysis of theoretical backgrounds, but it often overlooks the fact that the application of theory was happening within the scope of teacher associations, conferences, and during the normal operation of school supervisors. In this chapter, the author analyses the influence of Henrik Schreiner, headmaster of the Maribor Teacher Training College, that the pedagogic theory in the hands of performers got common-sense modifications which could be highly efficient and well received among innovatively inclined teachers. This additionally strengthens the necessity of regarding Herbartism from different perspectives.

Herbartianism cannot be treated as a monolith pedagogic paradigm, which has often been a failing of previous research studies. In the next chapter, we describe and analyses the disputes between the Catholic and liberally inclined pedagogues and their relationship towards Herbartianism, which at times became marked by ideological bias to achieve different purposes.

But we cannot overlook the fact that during the supremacy of Herbartianism, the school was subject to justified critique warning of its rigidity, formalism, intellectualism, etc. In short, it is impossible to ignore the fact that Herbartianism also contributed to the derogatory image of the "old school". Despite this negative impression, the last chapter shows that the image of the school was not so much connected to the weak points of the pedagogic theory as it was to the need of the state to oversee and direct lessons, which was accomplished with school supervisors.

# 1. Herbart's University Pedagogical Seminar[12]

How well new pedagogical ideas are actually implemented is ultimately dependent on how successfully future teachers and educators are trained. In contrast to the development of pedagogical ideas, systematic, scientifically grounded reflection on the concept of teacher training came into being rather late. Indeed, Herbart's contribution in this area can be seen as groundbreaking. Reconstructing the process of the formation of the concept of teacher training, which took place at the end of the nineteenthth and during the first half of the twentieth century in this part of Central Europe, an area under the cultural, economic and political influence of Germany, demonstrates that this concept was strongly influenced by Herbartians, i.e. those belonging to the pedagogical movements which based their doctrine on the Herbart's system and understanding of pedagogy as an academic subject (cf. Protner 2003). This chapter has three goals. First, it seeks to set out the historical framework with a description of the biographical context and organisational and systemic solutions with which Herbart established his pedagogical seminar. This serves as the foundation for an outline of some of the theoretical dilemmas Herbart faced. Special attention is paid here to the dilemma between public and private interests in the establishing of a school system–a question that still requires careful consideration today. Herbart's conclusions on the functioning of the university pedagogical seminar and the theoretical foundations on which it is based allow us to see Herbart in a whole new light, one quite different from the image depicted in older academic sources.

## 1.1. The Development of Herbart's Pedagogical Seminar

Kant's death in 1804 left one of the leading and most renowned chairs of philosophy, at the University of Königsberg, vacant. In 1808, when Kant's immediate

12 This chapter is an expanded and corrected version of an article first published in Slovene (Protner 1996), and later in English (Protner 2009a).

successor (W. T. Krug) accepted the professorship at the University of Leipzig, the leadership of the university was forced to find another professor, which was by no means an easy task to accomplish since prospective candidates for such a prestigious position were expected to meet extremely high standards.

When no one came forward to apply, J. W. Süvern (then Professor of Philology at the University of Königsberg, who a year later became a state advisor in the Department of Culture and Public Schooling in the Prussian Interior Ministry), proposed Herbart as a possible candidate (he had known him personally since before Herbart's arrival in Königsberg). G. H. L. Nicolovius, who was at the time a director of the aforementioned department (cf. Asmus 1970, 20), also agreed to the proposal. They were both enthusiastic followers of Pestalozzi who strived for reform of the Prussian elementary schooling system in the spirit of his pedagogy. They were convinced that Herbart, with whom the public were familiar through his essay *Pestalizzi's Idea of an ABC of Sense Perception Instruction* written in 1802, would be an ideal candidate to support their efforts (Ibid.). It seems to be generally accepted that Herbart's pedagogy played a greater role than his philosophy when the administrators of the university decided to invite him to Königsberg (naturally, he was also a greatly esteemed philosopher).

Herbart replied to the official invitation with a letter dated 24 October 1808, in which he very politely set as a precondition of his coming to Königsberg the possibility of establishing a small experimental school there. As Herbert explains: "Among all my occupations so far, the one I hold most dearly is my lecturing on education [Erziehungslehre]. Yet, it is not enough to solely lecture on these matters, but it is also necessary to demonstrate it and to practice. Besides this I would like to broaden my (almost decade-long) experience in this field. Therefore I have been considering the idea of teaching a smaller number of selected boys in front of a few young men acquainted with my pedagogy, who would later, at a certain point and under my supervision, try to continue the work progressively independently. This would gradually stimulate the development of teachers whose method would be implemented through the observation and exchange of experiences. Since no syllabus can operate without teachers, more specifically, teachers who are imbued with the spirit of the programme and who put it into effect with the use of the method, an experimental school as I imagine it would be the most appropriate method of preparation for the future realization of bolder ideas. In Kant's own words: First experimental schools, only then can we have model schools [Normalschulen]" (Herbart 1808/1982, 11). In this letter, he mentioned that such an experimental school would not merely serve his own personal wishes and needs, but would also prove beneficial to the local authorities (Ibid.). This indicates his readiness to take an active part in school reform, however, his ideas differed from those of the reformers (as we shall see later in this chapter).

Soon after Herbart's arrival in Königsberg the Department of Public Education entrusted him with the responsibility of realising the idea of an experimental school (a pedagogical seminar). Herbart began to do this by producing a *Draft for the Establishment of a Pedagogical Seminar* (cf. Herbart 1809/1982), which shows that he expected to benefit from this seminar in two main ways. He considered the most important result to be the systematic and controlled collection of information about the practical implementation of the pedagogical process, which would be linked to and complement general theory. On the other hand, he understood the pedagogical seminar as a centre for the education of future teachers, who in the spirit of his pedagogy would exert influence upon the reform of the public school system and education in general.

Herbart founded the organizational structure of the pedagogical seminar on the conviction that there was no right education in place at the time and that lectures on pedagogy alone could not improve the situation to any great extent. Herbart thought very concretely about the starting point of the future organization: For the takeover of the educational mission, one would first need to find a capable young man who was properly educated under advantageous circumstances and also search for a suitable family. The family (and not the classroom) should represent the centre of the pedagogical seminar in which future teachers would be taught. In accordance with his pedagogical theory he wrote: "Joining the educator invariably with hosts of boys (in a kind of institute, for example), means fathering a corporation instead of an individual, and to rob one of the most refined observation, and the most sincere attachment. This is not the way to develop one's true pedagogical feelings [.]" (Ibid, 14).

Herbart conceived the organizational structure of pedagogical seminar in the following manner: The educator would move into the house of the chosen family and take over complete responsibility for the upbringing and education of two boys aged between eight and ten years old. The parents were to be persuaded that the boys need a serried and uniform education, which would have to last at least six to eight years. In addition to this, the parents had to be made to understand that education carried out in the presence of observers (students of Herbart's lectures on pedagogy) is more effective and reliable than ordinary education. Accordingly, the educator's role is also to prevent any harmful influence that might be caused by the public (not more than six people altogether) on home upbringing and the life of the family in general.

The educator should set aside time for parent-teacher interviews, during which he would not only counsel the students but, importantly, also explain her/his behaviour in individual and particular cases of teaching and education in accordance with the objectives of the entire programme.

This educator would be expected to consult the public teacher of pedagogy (Herbart) on a very regular basis by considering "that both of them initially agree on the essential principles" (Ibid, 16). This does not mean that the educator should necessarily follow the teacher's advice when a difference of opinion occurs, yet he has to support his position professionally. Herbart certainly imagined that education in the pedagogical seminar would adhere to his pedagogical principles and he therefore precluded the possibility of any larger scale differences. In his own work, the educator should exercise and test out pedagogical theory and complement its foundation. Thus, one of his most important tasks is "to prepare an annual dissertation in which he uses his acquired experiences to elucidate on part of the theory" (Ibid.). This report would be handed in to the pedagogy teacher, who would then submit the paper with his remarks to the state board. The report would also be published for the general public.

It was thought that for the beginning at least two educators should be appointed, whose salaries would be paid by the government. Since in Herbart's opinion, the educator's dependence on the home where he would be placed would be an aggravating factor, he hoped that (within the framework of the seminar) a network of home teachers (paid for with public funds) would gradually take shape. In time, the initial home teachers would educate others, who would then pass their knowledge on, and so on. Gradually the state would have to contribute additional funds to those paid by the families for whom home educators worked, so that students would be able to attend their lessons.

The pedagogical seminar was to be based on the principles of home education, yet would also be followed by "the introduction of teaching methods shaped in the seminar to schools. This should not be prescribed by the state, but the state would have to allow the newly appointed teachers to bring their methods with them, and the old teachers would–on the basis of free choice [aus freiem Zutrauen]–also try it out. The state would sanction the school programme only when the majority of the most important members of the teaching staff freely chose to join, within the realm of the truly pedagogical school programme" (Ibid., 17-18).

The Department of Public Schooling accepted Herbart's draft and charged him with finding someone for the position of assistant (educator) for whom the state intended to provide financial means. Even though only half of the total funds Herbart envisaged for the two educators was approved, the Department "fully entrusted"

Herbart with co-ordinating the running and regulation of the seminar (Asmus 1982, 348). Because the external conditions were not appropriate and because the chosen assistant refused the post, the draft was not actually realised in the form Herbart described. In the next school year Herbart organized the Institute of Didactics instead of the pedagogical seminar.

## 1.2. Institute of Didactics

In the first report of the Institute of Didactics (Herbart 1810/1982), he explained his nomination with the claim that this Institution "is only concerned with the art of teaching and that other aspects of pedagogical training is being left out because circumstances do not allow" (Ibid., 18). His attitude towards this Institute can be seen from one of the later reports in which he refers to the substitution of the pedagogical with a didactic institute as an "emergency exit" (Quoted in Asmus 1970, 56).

The organizational scheme of the Institute of Didactics was the following: A defined number of capable students distributed among themselves the different subjects of instruction they wanted to teach. In addition, each of them sought out two or three boys (with the help of personal acquaintances) to teach for four or five hours a week based upon a previous arrangement with Herbart. They then alternately presented their individual lessons (with their own students) in front of other students. Every week there was a pedagogical lecture between these lessons in which Herbart presented particular aspects of education in relation to education as a whole. Those who performed the lessons were then given feedback. In his opinion, such an organization did not ensure complete integrity, yet such clarity was of significant help in the understanding of the theory that would follow in the next semester (cf. Herbart 1810/1982, 18-19).

In order for the work of the Institute to be more effective, Herbart proposed that the state appoint two assistants (students) who would receive a salary from the anticipated funds for the pedagogical seminar, which had fallen through. Their duty would be to improve their own knowledge and offer other interested students help with improving their skills.

The report was accepted and Herbart was authorized to continue putting his plans into practice. Herbart's annual reports on the functioning of the Institute were always readily accepted by the Ministry, moreover, the Ministry was convinced that the first draft was more appropriate than the second and therefore promised that (within the range of possibility), it would strive for its realization (cf. Asmus 1970, 94).

Mostly due to the lack of a steady stream of students, Herbart asked to be relieved of his duties in 1815, only to propose soon after—encouraged by a university curator in the appendix to the report—to extend the Institute of Didactics into an Institute of Pedagogy (cf. Herbart 1815/1982). In order for it to become a real pedagogical force" (Ibid., 21) that could meet the prescribed standards of the high-school leaving examination (Matura), the pedagogical professorship would have to be connected to the pedagogical seminar. It was thought that children of nine to 14 years of age should be the target age group, as this age group is pedagogically the most demanding in teacher training. "Boys of that age need home education or upbringing [Zucht], and education of that sort must be kept in one's hands if they are to be suitable as students" (Ibid.) of his Institute, which he envisaged as a kind of a residential school, numbering 12 (or in special circumstances a maximum of 20) students. Wealthy parents would pay for accommodation themselves, and some places for socioeconomically disadvantaged students would be provided by the state. First and foremost, Herbart called for the state to provide for an adequate house with a garden and for two teachers. Later Herbart presented the basic organizational and content scheme and the operational expenditure of running such an establishment.

The Ministry allotted him the expected funds on 15 March 1816 for the rental of the residence and the garden, as well as a retaining fee for the teacher and participants in the seminar. The rearrangement was finally completed in September 1818, because Herbart was unable to find a suitable house before that time. Eventually, he bought it with his own money (without taking advantage of the loan offered by the University) and lived there with his boarders and a teacher until his departure from Königsberg in 1833.

## 1.3. Pedagogical Seminar

During this time, the seminar operated in accordance with the *Draft of Regulations for the Pedagogy Seminar* (cf. Herbart 1821/1982), which Herbart wrote in 1821.

He imagined the pedagogical seminar as an institution for students, "where through transparency and their own experience the students would become acquainted with the most important and difficult elements of the art of education" (Ibid., 24), which would be indivisibly connected to the philosophical and pedagogical lectures. It would operate on a very liberal basis, as Herbart explains: "The principal of this institution must stick to (instead of the regulations which would hinder his work) two basic principles: the principle of subordination of pedagogical function to the academic vocation and the principle of the public nature of the seminar[.]" (Ibid.). He presented these points in the sixth article as the possibility of having one or two experts of his choosing (e.g. members of the university examination board), who would once a year attend the pupils' examinations as well as observe the seminar leaders as they worked. In addition, the two of them would also individually report on the operation of the seminar. Unannounced visits were also acceptable as long as they did not disturb the teaching process. If, however, visits by people from outside the pedagogical circle were to spread, they would have to be restricted to fixed days and times with the caveat "that the institution, though dedicated to shaping improved methods, nevertheless does not wish to disseminate teaching methods through their recurrent presentation; its primary function is the personal training of the seminar goers for teaching and educating. The value of a pedagogical approach can not be seen therefore in short-term observation, but only recognized through later long-term success" (Ibid., 24-25).

To run the seminar, Herbart envisaged two helpers who would be paid for their work. Herbart would reserve the right to hire and fire these paid employees. The first one would have the title of "Supervisor" and would live at the residence. He would oversee the boarding students along with the seminar participants and report on them to Herbart (or to the Director, as he is called in the text). Apart from this he would also teach (with a reduced timetable because of his youth and the need to complete his own training) and would be available to substitute for others. This position was to be filled by someone who had proved that they had above-average capabilities and had already finished or were just about to finish their studies.

The other helper would be called "Teacher" and would teach those subjects that the seminar participants were unable to teach. He would also be expected to stand in for them during the academic holidays.

In practice, the rest of the seminar participants were only supposed to teach certain subjects (according to the instructions and the rules set through pedagogy), yet they also had to be especially aware "that not one of them performs any separate work, and that the desired pedagogical education will have to be attained through a reciprocal and collective observation of that which will derive from their collective work, rather than out of the autonomous work of each individual…What they perform here on a smaller scale, they will later have to apply under broader circumstances" (Ibid., 26). Therefore, each individual seminar participant would always be allowed to attend the classes of another seminar participant, even if unannounced.

Once a week the seminar participants were supposed to meet with Herbart and present their pedagogical papers, and, at the same time, the methods of the results of their work. "However, the director may call a halt to the meetings immediately if it appears that there is not enough relevant material for a noteworthy discussion; nothing that happens in the seminar should ever slip to the level of pure formality" (Ibid., 26-27).

Herbart expected that the seminar participants display a high level of interest and motivation as well as a sound pedagogical, psychological and philosophical grounding. They were also expected to commit themselves to teaching their lessons for at least a quarter-year since their unannounced withdrawal from school could disrupt the integrity of the lessons as a whole.

Herbart defined the scope of the lessons and education briefly in two articles. As a rule, the classes in the seminar were to include the school materials and subjects of the grammar school from *Quinta* to *Secunda*[13]. This would enable that the pupils would be nine to 12 years old when entering school, making them eligible to enter the Prima or Secunda high school. In doing this, it was important that "their number…with regard to the number and capabilities of the seminar workers stays in such a balanced relation, as to keep the pedagogical power in the forefront… and that it is possible to be occupied with each pupil as much as it is required" (Ibid., 28). On the one hand, Herbart does not mention home or private schooling any longer, yet on the other hand, it is clear from the draft, and especially from his reports, that the seminar functioned on the principle of home education. This is a typical feature that fundamentally defines his entire pedagogical concept and is closely linked to his views on educational reform.

## 1.4. Herbart's Opposition Within the Framework of Educational Reform

In the introductory section to the *Proposal for the Broadening of the Didactical institute into the Pedagogical Institute*, Herbart wrote the following: "When I try to carry out this task…, I have to remind you, that our regal government rules for the purpose of being empowered to demand high standards and achievements in education; it does not want small establishments but aids the founding of bigger institutes. I presume that it is well known to our high Home Office (if not otherwise then certainly through the reports of the Scientific Deputation), how far our

13 According to Süvern's instructions from 1816, every general high school should be made up of a lower (Sexta, Quinta and Quarta), which lasts for one year; middle (Tertia and Sekunda), which last for two years; and higher level (Prima), which lasts three years.

schools still are from the goals we have set. I may presuppose with some certainty that the wisdom of my respectable superiors excludes the position that enforcing of the orders could substitute for the position of good teachers or the joy and love for science in schools, which is the only assurance of productiveness and is in direct opposition to passive learning [treibhausmäßigen Lernen], which can be satisfied only by *learned* teachers" (Herbart 1815/1982, 20, emphasis in original).

With this preface, Herbart reminds the ministry that his views on educational reform greatly differed to the direction advocated by the government. It is, however, interesting that in spite of this, Herbart commanded such a high level of trust and support. He clearly manifested his (partially) oppositional role within the sphere of the educational reform as early as 1810.

Herbart was not subordinated to the Department of Education only as a professor at the University, but also as a member (and for a time, Chairman) of the Scientific Deputation in Königsberg. K. D. Hüllman, the first Chairman presented (on Herbart's initiative) the *Draft for the Establishment of the Institute of Education of Home Teachers of the Province of East Prussia* to the Department on 23 May 1810 (Hüllmann 1810/1982); this happened when the Institute of Didactics was already in operation. The plan was formed out of two sets of circumstances: The extremely poor financial situation of the majority of students of theology, who sought open positions as home teachers, and the low quality of the schools where they received their first education. Competitiveness amongst them had so lowered salaries that in order to survive they had to sacrifice a substantial part of their day to teaching. A great number of them left for a definite period to the countryside to live with wealthy families, which prolonged and interrupted their study. However, Hüllmann stressed that the plan would not resolve this issue, but instead strove to improve private education, which was of poor quality specifically because educators alternated too frequently. As Hüllmann describes: "Besides that, how can those who are hired perform their one-day work simply for the sake of a day's pay, without any feeling for inner calling, for the development of spirit, for the betterment and deepening of the souls of their protégés, those who have no idea about the art of education, who are without teaching method, who are unprepared" (Ibid., 42). An improvement could be made by the Institute for the Education of Home Teachers, which would offer families in the provincial regions only those candidates "who have finished their academic studies and who would therefore as a rule not leave so quickly and who have acquired, through supervised and guided pedagogical practice, all the necessary preparations for this important work" (Ibid.).

Later in the plan it was stated that Herbart and F. A. Gotthold (a member of the Scientific Deputation and the director of one of the grammar schools in Königsberg) would take over the execution of this project as a private matter. The starting point for their project would be Herbart's Institute of Didactics, in the sense that those involved in this Institute (active students), who were expected to teach at the grammar school, would be trained as home teachers under the leadership of Gotthold, the Institute's Director. Every participant at Herbart's Institute of Didactics and the majority of those involved would become members of the Institute for the Education of Home Teachers. Families who sought an educated home teacher would turn to Herbart and Gotthold, while the families who did not do so would have to have this behaviour explained to them. It was thought, however, that such resistance could be avoided if the Institution were recommended by the clergy and educational authorities.

The Department of Education rejected this idea entirely. F. E. D. Schleiermacher, who was then a member of the council in the Department, wrote in his refusal dated 9 June 1810, among other things: "On the other hand it is somewhat inappropriate for the authorities to approve of recommendations being made on behalf of the private institutes. Besides it is very common practice for those who want better home teachers to turn to the experts. Those who have profited from Professor Herbart's Institute of Didactics or have had an opportunity to try their hand at teaching in Königsberg grammar schools have hardly missed out; being forced to search for vacancies as home teachers is an excellent way to find sanctuary and thus make themselves valued. And to devote particular attention at universities to the education of home teachers seems so much less advisable, as it is desired that with the perfecting of public teaching institutions this vocation will slowly disappear" (quoted in Asmus 1982, 368).

Herbart took his proposals regarding the organization of the Institute of Didactics or the pedagogical seminar and Institute for the Education of Home Teachers to the authorities as a public servant (a university professor and a member of the Scientific Deputation), who was involved in the state reform of the school system. It is certainly clear that the authorities supported him when they saw some benefit for the public school system, particularly with respect to the education of public teachers, yet they opposed his ideas for the education of home teachers because they were not in compliance with the envisioned reform. Although Herbart cooperated with the governmental authorities (and that they expected his help), he nonetheless did not believe that it was possible to change and improve the education and upbringing of youth on the basis of state educational reform. He presented his critical stance towards the reforms and public education to the members of the German society (therefore privately, and not as a public servant) on 5 December 1810 in the paper *On education under the public influence*. (Herbart 1810/1982a).

At its time of publication, the content of this paper was close to Schleiermacher's answer and can be seen also as an explanation as to where and in what kind of framework Herbart saw the role of home education.

When Herbart wrote in the preface to the paper: "Allow us first..., that those who explore the needs and potential of education are those men who consider schools from the viewpoint of the state and yet are aware that this is by no means the right way" (Ibid., 144), he surely had in mind the Prussian reformers of the education system (Humboldt, Süvern, etc.), although he did not name them. As early as 1792, Humboldt wrote the essay *Ideas for the Attempt to Determine the Boundaries of the Activities of the State*, in which he also advocated that limits be set on the influence of the state in upbringing and education; he also advocated this stance as a leader of Prussian educational reform during the years 1809–1810. His idea was based on the demand that general education be given precedence over vocational education. Out of this demand another one was grew– that there can be only one general education and that the school system must therefore be unified and horizontally divided by age. Of course, this means uniformity of schooling in the didactic rather than social sense: Parity of study subjects, of content and above all, of teaching methods. The struggle against the submissive mentality was also to be a feature of all educational institutions (cf. Blankertz 1982, 119-121).

Herbart was more aware than the reformers of the difficulties in the execution of the envisaged reform. For this reason, he wrote: "I maintain that the path from politics to pedagogy is the wrong path. On this path all we find is an ever finer and more detailed research on one's abilities, which anyone could accomplish, and on which we can individually tailor one's educational needs. We do indeed have one country, yet this is the unity of collaboration, possibly of different elements. And therefore we will need schools, which are both different and of all kinds, schools in which there are also numerous fraternities, a sundry style of school associations, all of which means: an unduly early separation of the world of the child according to state distinctions and an overly hasty designation of differences among people, instead of the desired mixing and uniformity" (Herbart 1810/1982a, 145). The general education advocated by the reformers of the school system would in Herbart's view only benefit the ever more powerful middle classes and simply serve to strengthen social stratification.

Out of his criticism of the politically guided reform of upbringing and education, or the attempt to carry out social reform by means of educational reform, Herbart indirectly criticized schools as public state institutions. As he explains: "In any case the result is much milder if we place pedagogy where she should be, on her own two feet, if we conceive of her as a beneficiary of each and every individual, who needs her help to become what one will want to become eventually. Yet at the same time our schools are disappearing; since every individual needs their own particular upbringing. Education therefore can not function as if in some factory –it needs to concern itself with each and every individual. If schools do nevertheless remain, then they stay as they are, as some kind of last resort, since there are so many pupils and so few educators" (Ibid., 146).

It is clear that Herbart envisioned pedagogy as an autonomous discipline, and later he supplemented this with the believe that politics cannot and must not be pedagogized. His criticism of schools is twofold. He first warns that a school as a state institution is only an instrument of the politicization of education and a means of the institutional subordination of pedagogy to politics. He then adds that state schools can also not fulfill the mission of education in the broadest sense of the word (cf. Benner 1986a, 275). He understood education as an art, as an autonomous activity ("One's own talents, abilities, exercises and indeed one's place in human society is indispensable to the artist of education" [Herbart 1810/1982a, 148]), and the duty of the state is to make this possible.

Herbart holds that education as art is only possible within the sphere of home education, and therefore, without this experience it is not possible to form a proper educator. This does not mean, however, that Herbart strove for the institutionalization of home education, especially not in the sense that the home educator would be subordinate and materially dependent on the students' parents. Later in the paper he states: "I have often and for years thought about the issue of where a skilled and educated teacher could place oneself after a long teaching career, to be able to live exclusively for his art…Some middle ground between a home teacher, who belongs only to the household and goes unnoticed by the state, and an educationalist, who is a public figure and is much too far removed from families and far too defined by one's responsibility to the state and had lost the freedom of an artistic life" (Ibid., 150). In order for the educator to be able to shape every individual for one self, he must not belong to either the household or the state. Herbart knew only too well the danger in home education becoming subordinated to the pride of a particular family in their standing, thus losing its public significance (cf. Benner 1986, 35). Herbart saw a slightly utopian solution to this problem in communal educators, who would take care of the children of several families. The families would guarantee the educator the greater part of his income, yet the educator would not be entirely dependent on them; he would be a sort of adviser, who would take responsibility for upbringing and selected lessons, while science lessons would be left to public schools, so that he could determine which subjects his protégés would have. In this way, education would "become at the same time public and domestic and would merge many of the advantages of one and the other mode. This institution [Einrichtung] would have to begin in bigger cities, in smaller ones it could continue, yet among country folk it would not be necessary for it to spread as an institution, or as a pedagogical spirit stimulated by the institution. In order to achieve this it (the pedagogical spirit) does not require any prescribed ways, it will find those single-handedly" (Herbart 1810/1982a, 151).

Only this paper and the latter citation have enabled us to understand the meaning and the purpose of Herbart's pedagogical seminar. It was meant as a starting point from which the spirit of new education would spread, naturally grounded in his entire pedagogical concept. It was neither intended for the training of state nor home teachers, but rather of professionally autonomous teachers; because his proposal was organizationally difficult to carry out, this was the most he could accomplish.

Herbart was aware that he would not be able to put his proposal into effect, yet he nevertheless believed that it was possible to at least partially carry out his ideas within the scope of the existing school system. He wrote about this in *Aphorisms* from the Königsberg times (Herbart 1875, 47–50). His thinking is linked to the paper presented above and deals with the question of colleges for modern science subjects [Realschulen]. The fact that these schools are separate from grammar schools is, in his opinion, only a result of the state being more interested in vocational than general education. He strived for the incorporation of the demands of particular secondary modern schools into general grammar schools; at first he demonstrated the model of school regulation that "[D]oes not expose the students to the danger of remaining uneducated[.]" (Ibid., 47). This is a similar model to the one already presented in the aforementioned paper, in which he drew on the difference between synthetic and analytical classes. Analytical classes are above all personal and therefore require a private tutor who can take care of that which cannot be provided by the school: "Yet, as the cooperation between a private educator and schools seem to belong more and more firmly in the category of wishful thinking, the more important the following question becomes; should schools not take care from the beginning at least…of a bigger share of synthetic classes?" (Ibid., 48). He was of the opinion that this sharing could be achieved in terms of both the content and organization of grammar schools (with parallel, vocationally oriented classes), which he presents later in the paper, where he concludes that: "[S]uch a grammar school–and this being its main point–will be the workplace for those and only those, who have previously practiced as private educators[.]" (Ibid., 49).

In order for grammar schools to do at least something for analytical classes, Herbart suggested the appointment of two or three so-called repeaters, who would not only teach within the range of normal teaching hours, but would also accept pupils for individual consultations and who would also, when necessary, cooperate with their families. Their work could not be accomplished by substitute teachers, because during the lessons they could not observe the pupils as accurately as required in analytical classes: Instead, they should devote their work entirely to synthetic classes. Analytical classes demand people who do not stray from the appointed teaching methods, who are on the other hand indispensable in synthetic classes. The seriousness and discipline required in synthetic teaching impedes the trust of the students towards their teachers. Yet even if this does not happen, Herbart was convinced that the fear felt by students when they answer their teachers can lead to failure.

Herbart answered the rhetorical question "where do we take the repeaters" with the following: "Exactly where do we find those who teach synthetically. Among the very best of the private educators" (Ibid., 50).

The interpretations of Herbart's work which emphasise that he sought to enforce a programme of home teachers are certainly true (cf. Schwenk 1971). In other words, he wanted the pedagogy of home teachers to be considered as a school pedagogy (cf. Blankertz 1982). While weighing up his criticism of public and private education, Benner's statement that Herbart's pedagogy is "neither a pedagogy of home teachers nor a school pedagogy" seems well stated. He further claims that it was not preferentially adjusted "to a certain vocational group, but rather it was aimed at free pedagogical practice within which there would be a share for families as well as schools, as long as they did not follow the privatistically or to an abstract universality adjusted goals and neither educate the individual for their future profession, nor for general profit (in the interest of the state)" (1986, 35). This issue remains unresolved and is still regarded as a problem even today.

## 1.5. Herbart and Herbartianism

After Herbart's departure from Königsberg, the pedagogical seminar ceased. In 1836, the idea of the seminar was revived by H. G. Brzoska, Herbart's former student in Königsberg and a professor at the University of Jena, who wrote an exhaustive study on the need for and regulation of a pedagogical seminar at the university. His idea was later made reality by K. V. Stoy, who was also a former student of Herbart in Göttingen, and a successor of Brzoska at the University of Jena. After Stoy's death in 1885, W. Rein became the pedagogical Chair at the University and also took over the seminar. The person who organized the seminar in Herbart's spirit and the ideas of Brzoska and Stoy in Leipzig was T. Ziller (cf. Rein 1907). Although all of those mentioned above appealed to Herbart's pedagogical seminar as a reference, they nevertheless did not take into account the principal founding element of his plan: The principles of household education and instruction. Instead, they linked the pedagogic seminar inseparably with the practice teaching school and the preparation of future teachers for giving lessons to the pupils en masse in the classroom.

K. V. Stoy, W. Rein and T. Ziller are known in the history of pedagogy as the most typical representatives of Herbartianism. This doctrine is very often linked to the weaknesses of the so-called "old school." Stoy was particularly influential, albeit indirectly, in strengthening Herbartianism in the then Austro-Hungarian territory (and thus also in the Slovene provinces). In 1876, on the basis of his experiences with the university pedagogical seminar, Stoy organized a pedagogical seminar for teachers of elementary education in Beilitz (Bielsko/Biała). The Director of the seminar, K. Riedel became a Director of the teacher training college in Troppauu and a school counsellor for the Austrian province of Silesia soon after this reorganization. From this position he could (on the basis of Stoy's ideas) exert a strong influence on the new regulation of the education of elementary school teachers within the framework of the State Law for Elementary Schools from 1869 (Gönner 1967, 153-154).

While appealing to Herbart, a pedagogical doctrine came into practice to which even he was already critical. In the review of Brzoska's previously mentioned study Herbart wrote: "Here we find alongside sound instructions about the work of the seminar participants also short assertions about the issue which lies at the very heart of the pedagogical seminar; even though the statements are short they are significant in meaning. This seminar should connect grammar schools [gelehrte Unterrichtsanstalt] and different civic schools including the institution in which pupils will be taught as they are in village schools (complete educational institution for higher and lower classes)...This greatness...wants most likely to stand in opposition to that smallness demanded from us. The bigger and more harmonious the connection between school and seminar, the less its peculiarity will be felt. The greater the need for education for children, the greater the pressure will be, the need which is felt in all schools which want to move forward with a movement that has already proved successful. It is impossible to leave a well-trodden path; instead of observing individuals, all man sees is the multitude" (Herbart 1836/1880, 272–273). One thing is certain: Herbart was definitely not a Herbartian.

# 2. Pedagogical Tact and Personality of the Teacher in the Herbartianist Concept of Educating Teachers[14]

We can completely agree with Groothoff when he finds that Herbart's pedagogy means "the first height of theory–of the professional–educator and teacher and their education and training" (Groothoff 1972, 97). Here it is sensible to differentially point out two aspects of his theory. On the one hand, it is a wholesome pedagogic system that represents basic expert knowledge. This kind of knowledge is offered by Herbart in, for instance, his work *The Science of Education; Its General Principles Deducated from its Aim*[15], where he points out: "What the educator should care for must lie open before him like a map, or if possible, like a plan of a well-built city, in which sets of lines having similar directions always intersect at exactly the same angle, and in which the eye finds itself at home without preparation. Such a map I offer here for the inexperienced[.]" (Herbart 1806/1896, 84; Herbart 1806/1982, 22). A reliable orientation can only be achieved with scientific reasoning: "Pedagogy is the science which the teacher needs for himself" (Ibid.); this is followed by the famous limitation and delimitation of the whole educational programme, which is concentrated in "the idea of education through instruction" (Ibid.).

On the other hand, it is a question of pedagogic formation of the future educator, i.e. the concept of education that should enable the pedagogic theory to become effective also in practise. How should a practitioner be trained to act in accordance with aims derived from the theory, i.e. science, in concrete reality? Herbart's answer to the question of the attitude between theory and practise is concentrated in its conception of "pedagogical tact" and in the opinion of Adl-Amini, Oelkers and Neumann, it is "[t]he only related concept which was developed in the history of pedagogy. A new attempt at solving the problem of interonection should be continued here" (1979, 47).

## 2.1. Herbart's Understanding of Pedagogical Tact and Formation of Personality

The concept of the pedagogical tact was presented systematically by Herbart mainly in his first lectures about pedagogy: *First Lectures on Pedagogy* (Herbart 1802/1982).

14 This chapter is an expanded and corrected version of an article first published in German (Protner 2003).

15 *Allgemeine Pädagogik aus dem Zweck der Erziehung abgeleitet* (Herbart 1806/1982).

This text is not only interesting due to Herbart's explanation of tact but also because it contains information about his concept of pedagogic education. The students were told in his first two lectures what he would like to achieve with the lectures, what effects he anticipated and where he saw possibilities to form the future educator. Here he told them straightforwardly (as will be described more into detail later on) that he wanted to achieve more with his lecture than only transmit knowledge–he also wantedto achieve a personal shift. This is why we are not as interested in the theoretical problem of the relationship between theory and practise here[16], but rather in those elements of the explanation of the pedagogical tact which enable us to put ourselves into Herbart's concrete formation of future educators.

Herbart first emphasised to his students the meaning of "philosophical prudence", which represents the basis of any scientific argumentation. After this, he introduced the concept of pedagogical tact: "But now it happens to even the best theoretician when he performs his theory…totally beyond his will, that there is a middle part between theory and practise, a certain *tact*, the fast judgement and decisions which does not always act evenly, just like rut, which must not brag (like an entirely executed theory *should*) to hold the real demand of the individual example, as a whole and exactly in strict consequence and in total prudence regarding the rule at the same time." (Ibid., 126, emphasis in original). The pedagogical tact is an essential characteristic of a professional educator, the measure of his competence is in "*how* this tact is formed in him/her–or in accordance with the laws expressed by the science in its generality, or not" (Ibid., 126, emphasis in original).

Despite this, concrete practise cannot fully and always act in line with theory that is general and unambiguous and therefore teaches "too much and too little" at the same time. We are talking about a crossing from science to art. Herbart knew the feelings of educators well because he had rich experience with them as a home teacher. He knew that every practicioner has "a way of acting which is first of all dependent on his feeling and removed from his belief, where his inner movement and expression is more in the forefront than his outside influence; the mental state is more exposed than the result of his thinking" (Ibid., 126). But at the same time Herbart knew that the "mood condition"[17] alone does not give the basis for trusting the educators work, that this work has to subordinate itself to rational and justified goals, but that the irrational relationship in education cannot be ruled

16 Oelkers finds that the tact which was thought out by Herbart as a mediator between theory and practise "does not transmit at all but assumes a constitutive differentiation[.]" (1975, 93).

17 *Gemüttszustand.*

out;it is only possible to cultivate it with the formation of *tact* which has central pedagogic meaning in the direct relationship with the learner. The meaning of tact is, of course, in the fact that the educator's work is also guided by theory and not a moment's inspiration, but it seems Herbart is more interested in the idea that the theory would not suppress what is most valuable in the relationship above: Spontaneity and authenticity of the relationship, which alone can enable the contact between two personalities and their mutual influence. Herbart's understanding of pedagogical tact can thus be connected to the thesis that "Herbart and the post-Herbartianist pedagogy which understands that the subconscious is more effective than the conscious and that the rational knowledge of educational motives of a teacher often lead to a lessening of his educational influence if not to its complete demise" (Medveš 1989, 241). Herbart's understanding of pedagogical tact leaves room for the explanation that the meaning of the unconscious in the pedagogical process was also made aware theoretically. Geissler, for example, finds that there are some basic rules from psychoanalytic thought already present in Herbart's teachings about the "mechanics and statics of the soul" (Geissler 1970, 64)[18].

It seems that Herbart is trying more, through the formation of pedagogical tact, to train the future educator for sustainability in educational activity than appeal to his educational mission. Herbart warns against exaggerated enthusiasm. Although he explains to his students that "the person has to internalize that observation which is related to dignity, meaning and main auxiliary means of education" (Herbart 1802/1982, 128), but at the same time, he warns them against the image of an educator who is "a companion on every step" or "guardian of a chained slave who robs the boy of freedom and vice-versa" (Ibid.). Pedagogic education is intended for overcoming "fantasies" of educators about the child and its future. The ideal is not projected on a concrete child; it is moreso the development of the educator's personality. The centre of Herbart's aspirations is not the training involved in using educational methods, which enable the teacher a direct influence on forming the child, but the training of educators to identify situations that have an educational effect. The power of an educator thus lies not in mastering educational techniques

18 Furthermore, some authors (e.g. Romano 1976 and Johnston 1974) point out that Freud studied Herbart very thoroughly. On the other hand, theoretical analysis enables very interesting possibilities of interpretation of Herbart, as shown by Javornik and Šebart (1991), for instance. A certain degree of caution, however, is warrentedhere. Oelkers (2001, 103) also points to the closeness of Herbart and Freud, when Herbart speaks of the "raising and falling perceptual masses" [steigende und sinkende Vorstellungsmasse] but finds that this problem is "essentially different from the 'return of the repressed'" [deutlich unterschieden von der 'Wiederkehr der Verdrängten'] (Ibid.).

and constantly practising them, but ensuring that the educational techniques would not have to be used. Herbart namely envisions the educator as a "wiseguide from a distance who can gain the pupil with deep reaching words and a strong behaviour at the right time and can without a problem let his development during games and quarrels with siblings, his own aspirations for honourable manly deeds, his own opposition towards examples of vices with which the world tempts us or warns us against, go their own way"(Ibid., 128).

Herbart wanted to presentsuitable words and behaviour to students in the scope of education from a distance. Here he explicitly pointed out (in contrast to some of his contemporaries) that he himself does not expect educators to sacrifice themselves for constant educational activity, because the educator would thereby "neglect themselves", which results in a situation where "the relationship between the educator and the pupil becomes forever forced, unnatural and inhibitory to the power of education itself" (Ibid.).

This emphasis denotes Herbart's understanding of the educator's function, which got lost with Herbartians. Although Herbart also counts on the enthusiasm and devotion from educators, he does not expect constant educational activity to influence and accomplish the educational goal. It seems that the goal of art, which is transmitted to students of pedagogy, is more the development of the awareness about the position of the educator than the pupil in the educational relationship: "Our science has to teach us art which educates mainly the educator himself on a higher level[.]" (Ibid., 128-129).

The meaning of the building of personality was more emphasised by Herbart in his next lecture where he paralleled pedagogical tact with the formed character. "There is a school of moral character and also a school of pedagogical tact. And there are sciences in both schools: morality and pedagogy. Both, if they know their duty, will work with their performances on the task of creating those essential beliefs in souls and strengthen them and raise them to live enthusiasm, which enable every tact gained in the future its right direction" (Ibid., 131). Tact is thus a category of personality that cannot be gained through belief, which would be a result of dogmatic adoption of a theory. Herbart stated the goal of his lectures in the citation. This was followed with the appeal to the students not to accept his views without reservation: "Let your attention help me [by achieving the set goal - E.P.], let it help me where I am wrong, even your doubt and the unencumbered and emphasised communication of your objections so that you can contribute a good deed to human education[.]" (Ibid., 131). Reflection and self-reflection are crucial to the formation of tact. Only thinking and doubt enable the development of tact, the basic characteristic of which is reacting without thought and decisiveness: "the educator should prepare for the phenomenon which await them and the situations they will enter with considering, thinking, exploring, science–not so much regarding their future actions in particular instances but most of all regarding their own selves, their psyche, head and heart for right acceptance, understanding, feeling and reasoning" (Ibid., 127). Herbart believes in the possibility of forming those qualities of educators which evade empirical quantification, which, in a sense, belong to the subconscious and feelings. But at the same time, he clearly understands the supremacy of emotions and drives in the context of the educational relationship. Accordingly, reason and heart have to be formed before the educational relationship even takes place.

What Herbart offers the students is a science that should predetermine their soul, reason and heart, but this is not sufficient for the final formation of pedagogical tact. Pedagogical tact can only be formed from the concrete contact with the child. "It is only in action where you learn art, gain tact, skill, habit, reliability; but also in *action* art is only learned by *those* who had learned the science beforehand, took control of it, formed themselves through it and determined the impressions which will be made on them by experience beforehand" (Ibid., 127, emphasis in original).

Thus, Herbart could not establish tact with lectures alone. For the students to develop the reliability of pedagogic action they would have to be also given pedagogic practise. This was achieved by Herbart during the university pedagogic seminar at Königsberg (see Chapter 1). Here, he developed the model of pedagogial education by testing and implementing his pedagogic-didactic theoretical basis. This seminar presented Herbartians (together with Herbart's complete theoretical opus) with a role model and inspiration for their efforts in this field. But Herbartians had other issues to deal with. Their problems lay mainly in the transmission of Herbart's theory into school practise. "Herbartians translated Herbart's Science of Pedagogy [Allgemeine Pädagogik] into school practise. This is their autonomous achievement" (Klingberg 1998, 124). They also continually warned against the narrowing and false understanding of Herbart (see Dietering 1908). The problem of the transformation of Herbart's pedagogy takes on an additional dimension when we remember that Herbart's pedagogy was mainly intended for training house teachers (cf. Blankertz 1982). The model of pedagogic education in his university seminar was conceived as a model of house education; in this form it was indirectly intended for the pedagogic formation of future secondary school teachers. But generally speaking, his seminar did not have anything to do with primary school pedagogy and primary school teachers, as we will see later on.

## 2.2. Herbart as an Advocate of Home Education and His Attitude Towards Primary School Teachers

When Herbart became school councillor and honorary member of the Consistory in Königsberg and the territorial school board in 1829, he presented the president a comprehensive report on the operation of his pedagogic seminar. He also presented his views on the basic organisational questions relating to didactics and school administration. He wrote here about the education of primary school teachers: "The seminars for teachers on lower village schools did have some problems; but nonetheless their organisation is rather simple because we cannot expect form these teachers a large extent of their own understanding, the point is for them to continue their work in a manner which had been shown to them. In contrast to this, teachers in higher education act independently[.]" (quoted in Asmus 1970, 220). The issue of understanding assumes craft skills of primary school teachers. Herbart wrote this during a time in which demands for a more challenging educational process of primary school teachers with a stronger academic background started gathering more force (Neumann and Oelkers 1984, 231). We can assume that Herbart did not support these demands and here his views were similar to those of Schleiermacher, who was one of the ideologists of the Prussian school reform who also started tackling the problem of educating teachers. Schleiermacher subordinated the education of primary school teachers completely to the practical needs of the organisational programme of teacher education, which was also passed. He removed pedagogy from the curriculum because he thought that theoretical pedagogic thinking does not belong in the teacher seminar. The entire work of the seminar was centred on the practice teaching school,[19] which was to offer model classes [Musterunterricht] and serve as teaching experiments for teacher candidates (cf. Driesch and Esterhues 1961, 100). Both classes and education in village primary schools were thought of as a craft to be performed with the help of a basic routine, which does not require theoretical knowledge.

Schleiermacher is highlighted here because there is an organisational school question in which he fundamentally differs from Herbart's views (see Chapter 1.4). Shortly after coming to Königsberg in 1808, Herbart organised a university pedagogic seminar, i.e. didactic institute which became very active after 1818, when

19 Schools where teacher candidates performed practical teaching performances and sat at teaching demonstrations. By law, every teacher training school had to have its own practise teaching school.

the operation of the Institute was moved to his own home, which he organised as a kind of boarding house (Asmus 1982, 350-351). Although Herbart's activity was generally supported by the authorities, a setback came in 1810 when, as a member of the Scientific Deputation, he submitted the "Draft for the Establishment of the Institute of Education of Home Teachers of the Province of East Prussia" (Herbart 1810a/1982) to the public education officials. Herbart's idea was completely rejected. Schleiermacher, who was a councillor at the Sector at that time, wrote among other in the rejection reply: "On the other hand it is somewhat inappropriate for the authorities to approve of recommendations being made on behalf of the private institutes.[…]And to devote particular attention at universities to the education of home teachers seems so much less advisable, as it is desired that with the perfecting of public teaching institutions this vocation will slowly disappear" (quoted in Asmus 1982, 368). As a public employee, Herbart cooperated the whole time with the authorities, who they also asked him for help, but he personally did not believe that it was possible to change and improve the education of the youth through a school system reform. Privately, not as a public employee, he presented the members of the *German society* [*Deutsche Gesellschaft*] with his critical attitude towards the reform of the school system and public education on 5 December 1810, in a paper titled "On education under the public influence" (Herbart 1810b/1982). This is a report in which Herbart critically refutes the political leadership of the reform of the school system and its association with the social reform and at the same time substantiates doubt in the educational power of the public state school. According to Herbart, "proper education" is possible only within the scope of home education. Only this experience facilitates the formation of a "proper educator": "Their proper schooling is gained by the educators by being home teachers…This is where the schooling of a real educator starts" (Ibid., 149). This is why it is not surprising that Herbart organised his pedagogic seminar as a boarding house model. In the above mentioned report, he writes that practical work demands "pupils or students in every case" (quoted in Asmus 1970, 221) and that there are three possible organisational approaches: A few boys can be taught part time, we can envision an organisation which reflects school order or boarding school order where the participants get "wholesome education". Herbart emphasises that he only tried the first and third variant. (Ibid., 221).

Herbart distinctively doubted that the school could perform the function of upbringing, because "school does not broaden, it narrows pedagogic activity to a great extent, prevents the attachment to individuals because students are present at certain classes in large numbers" (Herbart 1810b/1982, 149-150). The Herbartianist programme presumed the exact opposite: Institutionalised school education is possible and necessary. It is clear that during the transmission of Herbart's ideas into widescale school practise, conceptual discrepancies already arose during Herbart's lifetime.

When Herbart left Königsberg for Göttingen in 1833, the pedagogic seminar ceased to be active. Herbart did not reinstate it at his new workplace. The idea of such a seminar was revived by H. G. Brzoska in 1836 (see Chapter 1.5), one of former Herbart's students in Königsberg and a professor at the University in Jena, who wrote an extensive study on the need for and organisation of a pedagogic seminar at the university (Brzoska 1836). This work can be understood as one of the sources of Herbartianism because it was an institutionalisation of Herbart's ideas. There are already elements in this work that can be recognised as differing from Herbart. He wrote in the recension of Brzoska's study: "Here we find alongside sound instructions about the work of the seminar participants also short assertions about the issue which lies at the very heart of the pedagogical seminar; even though the statements are short they are significant in meaning. This seminar should connect grammar schools [gelehrte Unterrichtsanstalt] and different civic schools including the institution in which pupils will be taught as they are in village schools (complete educational institution for higher and lower classes).... This greatness... wants most likely to stand in opposition to that smallness demanded from us. The bigger and more harmonious the connection between school and seminar, the less its peculiarity will be felt. The greater the need for education for children, the greater the pressure will be, the need which is felt in all schools which want to move forward with a movement that has already proved successful. It is impossible to leave a well-trodden path; instead of observing individuals, all man sees is the multitude" (Herbart 1836/1880, 272-273). Here, Herbart wants to form an educator, the Herbartians a teacher. Despite the dialectical intertwining of both concepts, their differences reveal the dimension of Herbart's pedagogy that Herbartians were never able to grasp.

Herbart found the one thing without which it would be impossible to envision the education of teachers unacceptable: A school classroom is essential for this education. Despite his unfavourable relationship towards the seminar in which practical training took place at the tutorial programme, which was supposed to present a certain type of school for seminar participants to perform in front of a normal class under relatively realistic circumstances they would later face in their own work, it was this model which took hold. During the second half of the nineteenth century, it was further established in the university pedagogic seminars in Jena and Leipzig by K. V. Stoy and T. Ziller.

## 2.3. The Herbartianist Concept of Teacher Education

### 2.3.1. The Organisational Characteristics of Stoy's and Ziller's Pedagogic Seminar

Stoy defined 9 December 1844 as the "birthday" of his seminar. This is the day when the seminar school (practice teaching school) became a part of the pedagogic seminar (Bliedner 1886, 20). Ziller's "academic seminar school" began operating in 1862; its organisational appearance was very close to that of Stoy's (Metz 1992, 44-45). This organisational appearance can be thought of as a specific peculiarity of the Herbartianist concept of teacher education–it was based on the deliberate intertwining of theory, practise and critical reflection.

*The School Order of the Seminar School in Jena* [Schulordnung..., 1858], which was led by Stoy, envisioned three types of weekly meetings of teacher staff (§ 12):

"a.) *Paedagogicum*, where methodological, didactic and psychological topics were the main points of the daily schedule;

b.) *Scholasticum*, where mainly the issues of school services were discussed and

c.) *Practicum*, where the teachers of individual subjects were put to the test" (Ibid., 3). Later in the school regulations, "Sholasticum" (§ 19) and "Practicum" (§23) are described in more into detail. Within the framework of "Sholasticum", talks took place about everything connected with the function of school–the "Incipient" had the opportunity here to perform a lesson in the presence of other teachers. The demand at the end of paragraph is important; it states that the performed lesson "has to be thoroughly and comprehensively evaluated" (Ibid., 4). The school order of 1881 defined the evaluation of a lesson presentation more thoroughly in the article that denominated this activity as "Kritikum" and prescribed: "The Kritikum subjects the attempted lesson presentation to a thorough and elaborate evaluation. In connection with this, the probationer has to prepare a self-criticism, the appointed reviewer has to prepare a critique in written form" (quoted in Soldt 1935, 80). This is a framework for the organisational structure, which we can also see in Ziller's *Leipzig Seminar Book* (cf. Ziller 1874). Three forms of regular meetings were prescribed there (§11): "Theoretikum", "Praktikum" and "Conference". Theoretikum had a similar function to Stoy's Paedagogicum and Praktikum had a similar function to Stoy's Practicum. Here it was also prescribed under § 14: "for each *Praktikum* the director at the same time also appoints a critic who, at his own judgement, prepares an oral or written critique for the conference" (Ibid., 105). The Conference had two tasks: "First and foremost, general matters concerning school should be discussed" (Ibid.). In this function, the Conference would have the same role as Stoy's Sholasticum. The second part of the Conference dealt with "the debate on the weekly Praktikum… and also with the director's attendance at lectures" (Ibid.). This is thus the parallel to Stoy's Kritikum.

This organisational image where theory, practise and critical reflection are intertwined can be understood as a specific peculiarity of the Herbartianist concept of teacher education.

## 2.3.2. The Differences Between Herbart, Ziller and Stoy

This triad of Theoretikum, Praktikum and Kritikum (Prange 1989, 25) was analysed on the basis of Ziller's *Seminar Book* by Klaus Prange (1989) who found that this triad is not original (Ibid.), but that Ziller's contribution is mainly in substantiating the connections between individual stages, which reminds us of "rules of proceeding in jurdicial processes" (Ibid., 26) and connects with Ziller's judicial education. "The Theoretikum establishes the link with general rules in the preparation of a certain methodological lesson unit… the rule is transformed into useful regulations. The Praktikum works on the basis of these rules, empty spaces are filled ad hoc in the sense of general rules; in the Kritikum it is established and conclusively determined whether that what happened was (firstly) in accordance with the rules and (secondly) whether these rules were equal to the situation or if they would have to be changed" (Ibid., 37).

Under the influence of law, it is also possible to explain those characteristics of Ziller's pedagogy which came to be written in the history of pedagogy as "an example of devotion, orthodox narrowness and rigid dogmatism[.]" (Ibid., 20). On the other hand, Prange found that Ziller wanted a "possibility of pedagogic or at least didactic casuistry, i.e. such action which connects the instance and the rule in such a manner so as to rule about new instances on the basis of the ones before, broadening the scope of experience and enabling an additional reliability" (Ibid., 35-36).

Peter Metz supplements Prange with his finding "that this educational concept to a certain extent originates in Stoy and that the characteristics of arrangement with regulations can be explained directly with Herbart's pedagogy" (Metz 1992, 48). In his opinion, the basic difference between Herbart and Ziller is that "while Herbart judged the ambitious programme of scientific pedagogy factually and skeptically, Ziller argued the possibility of its realisation with reformist zeal and a kind of religious definite certainty" (Ibid.). It is hard to imagine that Prange would not be familiar with the pedagogic concepts employed by Herbart and Stoy in their pedagogic seminars. In the initial part of his article, he points out the differences between Ziller and Stoy and emphasises that Stoy is usually attributed as “a less rigid and pedantry derivation of Herbartianist programme” (Prange 1989, 23). It seems that Prange here is mostly interested in the exposition of the legitimacy and relevance of Ziller’s efforts to make the teacher use reliable and proven (scientifically justified) pedagogic approaches, because this is necessary from a standpoint of responsibility towards the child. It also enables the controlled supplementation of existing rules. The same efforts can be attributed to Stoy, although their pedagogy is very different. Unlike Stoy, who envisioned pedagogy more “large-scale”, Ziller believed that for achieving progress, “painstaking work on details is necessary” (Bergner 1886, quoted in Ibid., 39).

Ziller and Stoy had very different views on central Herbartianist categories such as formal steps, cultural-historical steps and concentration. Rotraud Coriand has convincingly shown the falsehood of “the impression that Herbartianism is mainly a closed and non-contradictory pedagogic discipline” (Coriand 1998a, 16; see also Protner 2000, 138, 372). The proximity or distance from Herbartianism are also not reliable criteria for judging whether something belongs to Herbartianism, which is nicely illustrated by two contradictory evaluations of Stoy’s attitude towards Herbart, which can be found in Herbartianist literature. Mostly critics of Ziller’s course were the ones who pointed out that he was less orthodox in relation to Herbart than Ziller (Bellerate 1980, 20). Wesendonck is, for instance, of the opinion that Stoy was “undoubtedly the most ingenious and practically most gifted” (Wesendonck 1885, 3) pedagogues among the Herbartians. Although Stoy was Herbart’s direct studfent “he did not follow Herbart’s words and regulations with such pedantry strictness as did Ziller, he was more after the spirit of Herbart’s ideas and gave the most emphasis on the personality of the educator” (Ibid., 22-23). We can agree completely with this opinion, although the suggestion is also present that the “pedantry strictness” when reading Herbart diminishes the significance of the educator’s personality. But we can read and understand Herbart in different ways. Thus, it is no surprise that Wilhelm Rein–Ziller’s supporter–described Stoy as follows: “Stoy is an orthodox Herbartian who abided by Herbart’s words and did not exceed him, while Ziller was a free improver of Herbart’s thoughts” (quoted in Bellerate 1980, 201). Two such different estimates of Stoy’s pedagogy lead us toward a conclusion that the understanding of the meaning of teacher personality and its formation within Herbartianism was different, which also results in a different understanding of the pedagogical tact developed by Herbart largely in the context of home education, Stoy in the context of school environment, and Ziller in the context of school lessons. The differences can also be explained by the theoretical incompleteness of this concept. In the opinion of Adl-Amini, Oelkers and Neumann, this concept was “already with Herbart more a creative idea than a category incorporated into the system[.]" (1997, 46). In his theoretical essays Stoy gave this concept even less systematic attention than Herbart. Nevertheless, as far as Stoy was interested in the preservation of the spirit of Herbart's ideas, this was also the extent to which he maintained a similar understanding of pedagogical tact. This is also confirmed by R. Coriand's hypothesis: "that Stoy's practise of school life presents a practical version of Herbart's thoughts about educational lessons" (Coriand 2000, 118) in which originated from the fact that Herbart connected the idea of educational lessons largely with home education and Stoy tried to compensate for the difference between home schooling and school education with specific atmosphere of school life. In contrast to Stoy, Ziller treated the concept of pedagogical tact even more thoroughly than Herbart, but he tried to realise Herbart's idea of educational lessons mainly in school lessons.

His breakaway from the spirit of Herbart's ideas and his orientation towards lessons are easily recognised in the concept of pedagogical tact, which divides itself into "educational and lesson tact [Erziehungs und Unterrichtstakt]" (Ziller 1864/1884, 195). An even greater deviation from Herbart can be seen in his differentiation between "routine tact [Takt der bloβen Routine]", which is "false tact [falsher Takt]" (Ziller 1892, 47) on the one hand, and "the right form of tact" which is "formed through theory, *rational tact*, which is preserved in accordance with its rational results, which acts with certainty in accordance with its regulations and methods and is also not supplemented during knowledge lessons by professional knowledge" (Ibid., 48, emphasis in original). Ziller maintains Herbart's argumentation, which exposes the leading position of theory. But the results of "Ziller's scientisticall [szientistische] revision of Herbart" (Oelkers 1975, 125) which is introduced by the distinction between the "right" and "wrong" tact "can be understood…in Ziller's educational-methodological propositions. Their prescription-like use rather thoroughly corresponds to the scientific demands of the theory… The methodology in form of prescriptions provides the observance of science and its demands as well as reliable action" (Ibid., 126).

It has to be explicitly pointed out that Ziller greatly stressed the meaning of forming teachers' personality, because this is not in accordance with the predominant stereotypes about him. The pedagogic seminar was supposed to develop within a participant "a real educational spirit connected with conscientiousness and the feeling of duty which proves loyalty to obedience through devotion to the idea of education…with one word, pedagogic interest which is power on its own right and will give them even more power, if it permeates their whole personality and is founded on the highest ethical-religious goals[.]" (Ziller 1864/1884, 203). But Stoy gave the emotional dimension of teacher personality incomparably more attention in his pedagogic seminar than Ziller. In Ziller's seminar, the possibility of discussing and asserting teachers' subjective feelings was made difficult from the start because Ziller's *Rules of Academic Pedagogic Seminar* determined that "*Theoretikum sets the norms under which actions should be taken and the next step has to be, as in any action, that of truly follow the norms and that the subjective notions and false habits do not hinder us*" (Ziller 1886/1979, 150, emphasis in original).

In Stoy's pedagogic seminar the subjective dimension of pedagogic activity was valued and got special attention. The detail from the description of the course of the Kritikum, as it is remembered by one of the participants, is also revealing: "The probationer has the right to first report on his lesson, to admit the mistakes which he is aware of and explains them. This happens in the written critique, which is read. If a student wishes to make a critique on his own work, he has to go deep inside his own nature and activity to get aware of the reasons and interconnectedness of imperfections" (quoted in Soldt 1935, 81). One of the reviewers evaluated the performance of his colleague as follows: "The effort of the probationer to study the material with his students in spirit and his subjectivity are worthy of every praise." (quoted in Bliedner 1886, 313). The spirit of Herbart's ideas can also be seen from this feeling for the significance of small details in personal contact.

But Stoy also presumes even deeper personality changes than Herbart: "The change which has to happen in the thoughts and psyche of the pedagogic beginner is very big[.]" (Stoy 1878, 417). For the Kritikum to achieve its goal, there has to be "religious devoted subordination to tasks, demands and ideals in reliability, patience, persistence and readiness for every possible formal notice and reprimand" (Bliedner 1886, 296) which probationers are subjected to by the director and colleagues. The purpose of Stoy's pedagogic seminar exceeds, by far, the efforts which Herbart strove for in teacher education. Stoy understands the pedagogic profession as a mission, which can be connected with his theological education. Jacobs finds that "Stoy's theology does not target the balancing out of pedagogy and religious pedagogy, but in contrast to Ziller's Herbartianism totally accepts pluralism of educational goals[.]" (Jacobs 1969, 69) but "Stoy's theology can be completely evaluated as an attempt to join Herbat's theological concept of 'Science of Education' [Algemeinen Pädagogik] with aspirations for education which is based on confessional Christian responsibility" (Ibid.). We pointed out earlier that Herbart did not expect sacrifice from the educator–he even warned against it. In Stoy's concept of pedagogic education within the scope of the university pedagogic seminar, the formation of a pedagogic personality ready to sacrifice itself for the cause is present at least implicitly. The formation of teacher personality is explicitly apparent in Stoy's concept of educating primary school teachers.

## 2.4. Stoy's Concept of Educating Primary School Teachers

In 1866, the priest of the Protestant community in Beilitz[20] invited Stoy to take over the management of a seminar for training primary school teachers they wanted to establish there. Stoy enthusiastically accepted the invitation; he saw it as an opportunity to influence the entire Austrian school system and guide the much-needed reform (cf. Bliedner 1886, 116). The seminar began in December 1867. Its organisational structure and theoretical foundation is explained in the book by Stoy titled *Organisation of the Teacher Seminar* (1869). Stoy's activity had a relatively powerful effect on the further development of primary school teachers training (see Gönner 1967, 153; Gönner 1969, 46-47; Teml 1974, 94), who defined the *State Primary School Act* on 14 May 1869[21] and the *Organisational Statute for Female and Male teacher training colleges* on 26 May 1874[22] with a distinctive qualitative improvement.

Stoy defined three tasks for the seminar: School (subject) education, pedagogic education and soul education. The book mentions neither pedagogical tact, nor Theoretikum, Praktikum or Kritikum. Despite this, we can identify the key characteristics of these concepts from the 11 points in which the basics of pedagogic education are presented. This idea of the pedagogical tact can be identified in its initial point: "The final goal of pedagogic education in the seminar is the highest possible skill and reliability in using pedagogic laws and identifying the needed pedagogic responses in individual cases" (Stoy 1969, 43). This skill has to be based on the well-built pedagogical circle of thought "which is influenced by the transmission of general pedagogy, didactics, history of pedagogy" (Ibid., 43); psychology (Ibid.) and logic are also needed (Ibid, p. 44). Here we can find those elements connected under the framework of the *Theoreticum* in his pedagogic seminar. This is followed by points 7-9, in which Stoy explains the organisation of practical lesson presentations of the seminar participants, which is similar to the organisation of the *Praktikum*. In the tenth point, Stoy prescribes conscientious preparation for the presentation. In this point, he also demands that seminar taker, upon completion of their presentation gives "*a report* about their practise in the form of a self-critique, and from the individual seminar takers who were appointed

20 Today, this is located in southern Poland and is called Bielsko-Biała. At that time, it belonged to the Austro-Hungarian Monarchy.

21 Das Reichsvolksschugesetz vom 14. Mai 1869.

22 Das Organisationsstatut für Lehrer-und Lehrerinnenbildunganstalten vom 26. Mai 1874.

to evaluate the presentation and also from the other participants, exemplary teachers and the director of the teacher training college a thorough *critique*, the needed direction and help" (Ibid., emphasis in original). Here we can identify the Kritikum. The eleventh point, which prescribes that which was called the *Scholasticum* in Jena, also corresponds to the principles used in the university seminar.

The organisational structure of the seminar far exceeds the level of teacher education envisioned for primary teachers by Herbart. Here Stoy's contribution, along with the Herbartians towards the advancement of the professionalization of teaching is exceptional–this contribution cannot be limited solely to pedagogic and didactic theory. In Herbartianist theory of teacher education, we must distinguish between two dimensions: On the one hand, Herbartianist pedagogic theory was gradually being established as professional knowledge in terms of the content of teacher education and pedagogic practice. On the other hand, the Herbartianist concept of teacher education was established in the organisational structure of the seminars, i.e. teacher training colleges.

Stoy transformed the model of the university pedagogic seminar for theologians and high school teachers into a model for educating primary school teachers. This transformation was naturally not possible without quantitative and qualitative changes, and it seems that the education of primary school teachers–at the cost of a less intensive study of pedagogy as a science– was more exposed to the formation of teacher psyche. Deviation from Herbart can be best seen in these comments by Stoy: "The task of educating teachers is very great, like the weight of the demands which are intrinsic to a real teacher; they flow into one meaningfully rich word: *self-denial*." (Stoy 1869, 26, emphasis in original). This idealisation of the teacher profession is nothing new in the history of pedagogic thought–it has been present since Comenius. The novelty, which we can attribute to Herbartians, is that the formation of teacher psyche is no longer dependent on appeal and constraint. Herbartians establish an "intentional, systematic education of teachers" (Ibid., 27) and in this respect they were original. Herbartians were original in this point. Essentially Stoy preserves the typical Herbartianist thought structure, because the formation of the psyche "cannot be thought separate from the formation of the thought cycle…Thus, lessons are the first and main factor in forming psyche" (Ibid., 78). To make suitable "feelings, moods and direction", we also need "institutions and customs" which enable "gaining that discipline parallel to lessons with which the seminar enables the gaining a deep influence on the psychological development of students" (Ibid.). The aforementioned institutions and customs integrate life in a religious, cultural and social context–religious celebrations and state holidays, physical education, excursions and other special days in the framework of the seminar also belong here. One of those special days was the 17th of February, when scholarships were awarded. The day is significant because marks Pestalozzi's death (Ibid., 87). The leaning on the Pestalozzi's pedagogic cult (Osterwalder 1996) can also be understood as a Herbartianist revision of Herbart. The image of Herbart as role model in creating the psyche of primary school teachers could not be of help to the Herbartians.

# 3. Herbartianism in Slovenia Until the First World War[23]

Although Herbartianism belongs to one of the most established and attention-grabbing concepts of modern pedagogics, it is more and more evident that we cannot find a study in contemporary as well as older pedagogical historiography that would treat this concept thoroughly enough. Only a handful of studiesand presentations on Herbartian authors and individual Herbartian ideas and their characteristics can be ascribed to objective basis and evaluation. Despite the time that has elapsed, Herbartianism is still filled with stereotypical notions present in general pedagogic and school histories since the 1920s (cf. Oelkers 1989, 99). These are stereotypes formed within scope of the critique of the school system during the turn of the century, which constantly stress schematism, formalism, intellectualism, etc. The representatives of new pedagogic disciplines (mainly reform/ progressive pedagogy) have succeeded in attributing it negatively. These stereotypes have persisted; this is probably the reason it has not gained real interest until today. Herbartianism thus has to be judged more objectively; this does not mean that it must be rehabilitated or defended, but its evaluation and scientific judgement ought to be based upon similar criteria as, for instance, modern evaluations of reform pedagogy.

Research and knowledge about Herbartianism is particularly lacking in Slovenia. In general, understanding of Herbartianism is limited to what is discussed in the main Slovene textbook on the history of pedagogic ideas: Žlebnik's *General History of Pedagogy* (1978). Here Herbartianism is only mentioned in passing in the chapter about Herbart (and even here it is not named), where it says, "that some of Herbart's students ventured even more into the template conception of the make-up of the education process as Herbart himself[.]" (Ibid., 162). Among "Herbart's most zealous students", only T. Ziller is mentioned as the one "who brought Herbart's formalism to its peak and evolved it himself to an impossible extremity" (Ibid., 166).

Here we would like to point out some observations on the spread and general characteristics of Herbartianism and to focus mainly on the description of three

23 This chapter is an expanded and corrected version of an article first published in Slovene (Protner 1998).

development periods of the affirmation of Herbartianism in Slovenia from 1869, when the third Austrian Primary School Act was passed, until World War I. The discussion can be understood as the introduction to more thorough research on Herbartianism in Slovenia, which is essential for a more comprehensive understanding of this part of national history. Greater attention will also be devoted to Herbartian (and Herbart's) pedagogic theory because it represents a phase in legal development (and not a sideline) of modern pedagogy.

## 3.1. Dimensions and Characteristics of Herbartianism

There is a predominant belief in pedagogic theory that Herbartianism was a dominant pedagogic stream in the second part of the nineteenth century (and also first decades of twentieth century); it fundamentally influenced the character of primary schools during that time, and helped shape the professional image of the teacher[24]. This belief is accurate, but can be misleading because of its generality, especially if, as this is often the case, the weaknesses of the so-called "old school" are simply ascribed only to Herbartianism or even Herbart himself. Historically, school practices were mainly developed by school supervisors, who would adjust pedagogic theory to suit the interests of state. These were the individualswho imprinted Herbartianism with the characteristics that would gather harsh critique at the turn of the century. It is also reasonable to distinguish between Herbartianism and Herbart's pedagogic system. The leading representatives of Herbartianism (especially K.V. Stoy, T. Ziller, W. Rein) formed a firm and (for that time) attractive pedagogic theory while referring to Herbart's philosophic, psychological and pedagogic ideas, which deviated from Herbart's initial ideas due to their along with attempts to find greater practical application, and from the influence of other

24 Blankertz's claim is characteristic. He states that "Seminars for training teachers in the last third of the century was almost exclusively dominated by Herbartianist teachings about formal steps" and that "also primary school lessons and the professional self-understanding of the teachers was influenced by Herbartianism throughout the first half of the century." (1982, 155). One of the rare theorists who evaluates the influence of Herbartianism more carefully is Oelkers, who is of the opinion that the influence is very hard to estimate and that there are no accurate data regarding this subject at present. Despite this, he also establishes that the influence can be clearly identified in the practical expert literature of the time and adds that it was greater in the Protestant and urban areas of Germany than in the Catholic and rural areas (Oelkers 1989, 104).

social, political and cultural circumstances[25]. An overlooked fact is that these deviations were determinedly pointed out by some Herbartians who did not identify themselves with the dominant line of thought associated with Ziller, and later, Rein. Herbartianistic pedagogy had very strong opposition among its ranks; its leading representative was Stoy, who pointed out the unacceptability of Ziller's and Rein's teachings on culture epochs and the concentration center of lessons. Schematism and formalism of the teachings of formal steps were also rejected[26]. This was a group of people who inserted similar reproaches into this critique as they did in reform pedagogy and other pedagogical currents later on. In doing so, they still referred to Herbart. Although Ziller and Rein were the most influential Herbartians, their original teachings were not rooted in school practise. Their critics were active all the time, and their reservations were known to a wider circle of teachers. The question remains unresolved as to how large the share of individual currents of thought inside Herbartianism in forming school practise were. Here, we also must take into account that school character was also influenced by other pedagogical concepts. At least two concepts should be mentioned: The concept of the traditional Christian pedagogy and the liberal concept, which was strongly opposed to the former. The most prominent representative of the latter concept was F. Dittes, who is often referred to Pestalozzi and Diesterweg in his works. Under the political and ideological background of individual pedagogic concepts, Herbartianism can be placed between both of the above (cf. Franković 1961, 175)[27].

25 A more detailed analysis of the differences between Herbart's theory and the theory of Herbartians (especially Ziller's and Rein's) was performed by B. Schwenk (1963). General results of his analysis focus on the finding that Herbart's pedagogy was far less stiff, dogmatic and mechanistic than the pedagogy of Herbartians.

26 Very insightful is Richter's (1887/1908) analysis of Ziller's teachings on the formal steps, which illustrates all the radicalism of the opposition inside Herbartianism: "The effort to prescribe everything into the smallest detail, argue and derive from general principles has led to a petty school craft [schulmeisterlicher] pedantry, to dead and suffocating schematism, to utterly unnatural artificiality, to almighty dialectic artifices and shiny virtual basis…general truths are challenged and refuted, the thoughts right in their own sense are twisted with exaggeration, proven didactic rules are made infeasible with pedantic rules" (Ibid., 177).

27 Franković (Ibid.) cites F. Basariček's report on the proceedings on the meeting of German teachers in Hamburg in 1870, in which he identified four streams: cleric; progressive (followers of Pestalozzi and Diesterweg) whom he attributes a healthy eclecticism; radical (which formed in the scope of Beneke's psychology and advocated complete independence of school from church, whose representative was Dittes); and Herbart's conservative stream.

The question to which extent other pedagogic concepts influenced school practise would have to be investigated more in detail. The assessment that Herbartianism dominated school practise of that era is essentially supplemented by the fact that it never (except in rare private Herbartians schools) established itself as a complete, internally coherent theoretical and practical concept which could generate the intended results if school practise were to integrate all elements of the theory in its mutual correlation and co-dependence. In essence, it involves elements defined in a well-chosen manner by Fröhlich, as follows:

"**[O]ne** goal (goodness or character strength of morals),
**two** auxiliary sciences (ethics and psychology),
**three** main parts (government, instruction, discipline),
**four** formal steps (clarity, association, system and method),
**five** practical ideas (inner freedom, perfection, benevolence, right and requital),
**six** types of interest (empiric, speculative, aesthetic; sympathetic, social and religious)" (Fröhlich 1883/1901, 210, emphasis in original).

Without individual elements, the Herbartianist concept does not function completely and is not effective. This was actually an alternative pedagogy and the question is whether it could exist in the state public school system in such a form. Herbart himself opposed state regulation of education (see Chapter 1), and Ziller (1864/1884) also had similar ideas. Apart from this, Herbartianism evolved from its inception and asserted itself on the basis of the critique of inadequate educational work in public schools. Hermine Maier's finding is interesting in this context, namely because it was mostly the opponents of Herbartianism who claimed that Herbartianism dominated German schools in the second half of the nineteenth century. Herbartians were of the opposite opinion. T. Fritzch, for instance, wrote in 1922 that "German school unfortunately was not under the domination of Herbartianism. Not one public school could be organised under Herbart's, let alone Ziller's principles. The authorities made sure of this when they warned against this pedagogy in their circulars and decrees" (quoted in Maier 1940, 153). Maier confirms this opinion: "The German school…was never equipped with Herbart-Ziller's study programme. These characteristics were only present in workbooks in Jena and Leipzig as well as Franke's institutions in Halle under the supervision of O. Frick" (Ibid.). In her opinion, the spread of Herbartianism can only be discussed in limited scope. On the other hand, she also warns against overlooking the "internal convincingness with which Herbartianism managed to set scientific foundations of the German school and permanently influence school work and methods. How else are we otherwise understand the hard struggle which was inflamed with Herbartianism if it did not, in its core and spiritual sense, perform a long-lasting dominance" (Ibid., 154).

When discussing the influence of Herbartianism on the image of primary school, it is reasonable to point out also another element of this influence, namely its impact on the professional image of teachers. For practising teachers, Herbartianist theory of lessons and education was very attractive because it improved their professional self-confidence and class consciousness, while drawing on scientific foundations. It also helped form a very characteristic concept of teacher training in the scope of Herbartianism, which intentionally enforced this self-image (see Chapter 2). Within Herbartianism, the pedagogic theory and concept of training teachers were mutually related but were not incorporated side-by-side in school practise. On the basis of the comparison of Herbartianist concept of teacher education and legally prescribed organisation of teacher education in the Austro-Hungarian Monarchy after the passage of the *State Primary School Act of 1869* [*Reichsvolksschulgesetz* 1869], it is possible to deduce that Herbartianism co-shaped this organisation even before Herbartianist theory of education and lessons was recognised in the education of teachers. Although there was a very recognisable Herbartianist influence on the organisation of the education of teachers, this organisation was nevertheless shaped by other pedagogic concepts and, naturally, political interests.

## 3.2. The Period Between 1869 and 1890

Slovenia's expert pedagogic periodicals feature Herbart's name for the first time in 1872 (Vpeljava v zgodovino, 275), and later in 1877 (Ciperle, 115). Both times he was mentioned more indirectly as a famous philosopher, not as a pedagogue. Only as late as 1878 can we find an article in which the author quotes Herbart's pedagogic views, but they are explained in a manner that shows he simply did not understand them (Pokorščina 1878). In these years some (rare) articles were written in which we can see some elements of Herbart's pedagogy, but do not quote sources or systematically summarise pedagogic theory. Herbartianism's obscurity in Slovenia can be clearly seen in an article from 1885, in which an anonymous author mentions Stoy, who was, in his opinion, "a strict Herbastian [sic] and as such spread the principles of Herbast's [sic] pedagogy" (H.P. 1885, 107). Because the mistake is repeated twice, it is clear that the citation is not a typographical error regarding the misspelling of Herbart's name. This article features the first occurrence of the term Herbartianism, but in a way which leads us to believe the author knows nothing about him (he cannot even spell his name correctly) and that he probably does not connect the term with Herbart, even though his name was probably very well known to every student teacher. We can assume that it is a translation or summary from a foreign newspaper. When Herbartianism was, in the opinion of some, at its peak in 1885, it was not known to the Slovene pedagogic press as the most powerful or even dominant pedagogic discipline, even among those who published papers[28].

Only as late as 1887 can we find the first evaluation of Herbart's pedagogic work (Lapajne 1887), which, although short, is concrete enough. This article was published in Lapajne's *History of Pedagogy*, in *Učiteljski tovariš* [Teacher Comrade] (Ibid.). In the same year, F. Gabršek (1887) also published a series of articles on the educational function of individual subjects in the publication *Učiteljski tovariš*, which show the author knew Herbartianist theory. Although Gabršek never referred to a unified pedagogic concept and did not cite any of the characteristic Herbartians, his initial words prove that he was one of the first in Slovenia to perceive the appearance of Herbartianist pedagogy in the world. He states: "It is becoming more and more evident that one of the most abundant educational means are the lessons themselves" (Ibid., 17).

Gabršek contributed even more to the appearance of Herbartianism in Slovenia with the translation of J. Mich's (1887) *General Educational Theory*, a textbook for schools, which was published in 1887 and *General Didactic Theory* (Mich 1888), which was published the year after. These textbooks summarise the entire Herbartianist pedagogic system. Gabršek can be considered the first Herbartian in Slovenia, but this gives the impression that he did not consciously, reflectively implement Herbartianist theory. The fact that he chose such distinct

---

28 The debate is limited to the Slovene press only. Despite this, we have to mention that in 1884 there was a short article published in *Laibacher Schulzeitung* (the journal was published in Ljublana in German) titled *To Herbart-Ziller-Stoy's didactic principles* [*Zu den Herbart-Ziller-Stoy'schen didaktischen Grundsätzen 1884*]. In the introduction, the author stresses that scientific pedagogy (as Herbartianism was termed at that time) is winning more and more recognition and that familiarity with the events on this field is necessary for all teachers. He summarises Bartel's theses about how much Herbartianist pedagogy is useful in primary school practise. Bartels strived for a more in-depth study of Herbartianist pedagogy and the introduction of some of its principles in school practise, at the same time he pointed to the one-sidedness and exaggeration, especially in connection with the idea of concentration and culture epochs. He distinctively recommended the use of formal steps, but in as free form as possible. Although this article points to the familiarity of the author with the current events on the field of pedagogy abroad, this trade press did not feature articles which dealt with Herbartianism in detail either before or for some years after.

Herbartianist textbooks can be attributed more to his pragmatic judgement than to his professional-pedagogic judgement that Mich's (Herbartianist) pedagogy was professionally the most acceptable.

The analysis of Slovene academic journals to date shows that Herbart emerged and was established as an important pedagogue in broader circles as late as 1887. Except for indirect mentions of Stoy's name, there are no other Herbartians named. Herbartianism as a complete pedagogic system, which was already much discussed and problematized, was still unknown in Slovenia. This shows how much Slovene pedagogy lagged behind the times. But this does not mean that Herbartianism was not present. Slovene teacher training colleges used G. A. Lindner's textbooks for teaching about *Science of Education* (Lindner 1877) and *Science of Didactic* (Lindner 1877a), which covered (similarly to Mich) all essential elements of Herbartianist pedagogy. Lindner was considered the leader of the opposition against Ziller's discipline inside Herbartianism. This especially expressed itself in the way that he dedicated only a few lines to formal steps, teachings, which outset all other elements of Herbartianist pedagogy in his didactics; Ziller's idea of concentration was mentioned only as one of the possible forms, the concept of culture epochs was not mentioned at all. Despite this, Lindner also quoted other Herbartians apart from Herbart himself. That Slovene pedagogy lagged behind the times is further supported by the fact that teacher candidates were better and earlier acquainted with Herbart's ideas and ideas of Herbartians than the academic community. In terms of academic and scientific content, Lindner's textbooks were far more up to date than the pedagogic theory published in the SloveneSlovene scholarly press.

Despite this, we can assume that teacher candidates also did not consciously understand the knowledge gained from the textbooks mentioned as knowledge that could be connected to a certain pedagogic discipline. Herbartianism became consciously present in broader Slovene pedagogic circles only after it had to be defended against attacks (this also indicates how Slovene pedagogy lagged behind), which did not come from pedagogic circles, but from the Church. In 1890, A. Mahnič (1890) sharply attacked Lindner's pedagogic textbook in the publication *Rimski katolik* [Roman Catholic] with the accusation that it was anti-religious. Mahnič's critical basis was the argument that the subject of philosophy is most important in the formation of views of future teachers, which is present in teacher training colleges in pedagogy. In connection with this, he stressed that Lindner's textbook was most present at Austrian teacher training colleges. He joined his basis for critique with the finding that the textbook was based on Herbart's viewpoint. Mahnič had found that "…the state obligatory philosophy in Austria…is already known to all the world… [it]is Herbart's" and continued

"Herbart is one of many students of Kant. It goes without saying that he is a rationalist. Rationalism is generally against any positive religion. Therefore, away with religion in education!" (Ibid., 155).

Mahnič attributed Lindner's (and Herbart's) pedagogy a liberal political background and in this sense, he attacked the anti-religious, liberal orientation of the *Union of Slovene Teacher Societies*[29] in Ljubljana (Mahnič 1890a). A argument (Mahnič 1890b, 1891, 1891a; Romih 1890, 1891) started when T. Romih (the president of the *Union of Slovene Teacher Societies*) asserted that liberalism does not oppose Christianity. He also argued that Lindner cannot be blamed for having an anti-Christian standpoint. This viewpoint was decisively disputed by Mahnič. We have to admit that Mahnič's had a very in-depth understanding of Lindner's system of thought; his critique and explanation were, from the viewpoint of dogmatic Chatolic teaching, consistent and systematic. Unfortunately, Mahnič connected his broad knowledge with feisty performances and a fanatic search for heresy, thus undeniably extending the divide between the members of the liberal and clerical side.

Mahnič was also as well versed in Herbart's school of thought as Lindner's. It is still true today that Mahnič was one of the few in Slovenia who read, thoroughly studied and cited Herbart from the original source, which is evinced in his debate on Herbart (Mahnič 1893), which was also intended as a critique of Henrik Schreiner, the headmaster of the teacher training college in Maribor who, shortly after taking the position of Headmaster, became the leading pedagogic authority in Slovenia. It was first introduced to the broader professional public with a talk titled *Newest Aspirations for Reformation of the Pedagogic Field* which, presented at the 5th assembly of the association *Union of Slovene Teacher Societies* in Maribor in 1893 (Peta skupščina..., 1893). This talk could be considered a turning point in the development of Herbartianism in Slovenia.

## 3.3. The Period Between 1893 and 1901

Shortly upon taking the position as headmaster at the Maribor Teacher Training College in 1890, Schreiner started publishing in Slovene scholarly journals. He published a paper in 1892 that contains the idea of concentration in a characteristic Herbartianist sense (but not Ziller's) for the first time. He also advocated for the use of formal steps in lessons. Schreiner closed the debate with the assertion that it is vital to make exact syllabi for individual schools. Here there is a need to base

29 *Zaveza slovenskih učiteljskih društev.*

the methods on special methodologies of individual subjects that define how and under which principles one is to select and divide class material. The idea of concentration demands that the classification of the subject matter takes into account related subjects and that the subject matter is combined in stated groups (Ibid., 23).

It is obvious that this is Schreiner's text for publication of the lecture written for the assembly of the teacher society *Teacher Society for the Maribor District*[30] at the end of 1891. After his lecture, two decisions were made:

"a) To work towards the goal where lessons on our schools are in time constructed on the basis of concentration.

b) To create meaningful detailed syllabuses for all categories of schools of our district on the basis of local studies" (Maribor 1891, 341).

Schreiner is responsible for introducing Herbartianism as an independent pedagogic school of thought in Slovenia's scholarly circles and at the same time setting new, higher scientific criteria in pedagogic debates. Under his leadership, the Teacher Training College in Maribor became a centre of innovation for the entire region of Slovenia, particularly as a centre of study and implementation of formal steps in school practise. Here, teachers from the practice teaching school also played an important part. In 1891 G. Majcen, an instructorat the practice teaching school at the Maribor Teacher Training College published in a text (Majcen 1891) which represents the continuation of the theoretical argument for the teaching preparation printed before (Majcen 1891a). This was the first explanation of the teachings of the formal steps, which at that time called teaching representations. The publication was also significant in that it Slovenementioned Ziller and some other authors whom he classified as Herbartians for the first time in a Slovene pedagogic journal. Apart from Mahnič, who was not a pedagogue, Majcen was the first writer who publicly acknowledged Herbartianism as a complete and unified pedagogic discipline. It is an excellent text in which we can find great control of basic categories of Herbartianist psychology and didactics as well as the critical distance that enabled him to build a reasonably independent concept of class execution on the basis of the formal steps. Majcen was especially critical towards Ziller, his followers and some strict Herbartians. Although he did not associate himself with Herbartianism (quite the opposite), his concept was nevertheless recognisably Herbartian, similar to the ideas of those Herbartians who constituted the opposition within Herbartianism. Majcen's article shows that Herbartianism, which took time to gain momentum in, also included a reflection of the polemic critique that had been forming abroad for a whole decade before. This is also

30 *Učiteljsko društvo mariborske okolice*

similarly true for Schreiner. Slovene pedagogy skipped this phase in the development of Herbartianism with his arrival and indirectly entered modern pedagogic trends. Schreiner's lecture can be thought of as the foundation of this integration.

In this 1892 lecture, Schreiner attributes Herbart with the founding of scientific pedagogy and asserts that a new phase in the history of pedagogy began with him. At the same time, he reminds teachers not to teach directly according to Herbart and distances himself from Herbart's psychology, which he found to be false. Despite this, it is evident that he put Herbartianism under the framework of the newest reformatory aspirations on the pedagogical field, as he later adopted the basic ideas of Herbart's pedagogy and aligned with the presentation of *concentration* as understood by Ziller, Rein, Pickel and Scheller. His attitude towards their ideas was the following: "The subject matter of all other subjects is arranged around the lessons of world view [Gesinnungsuntericht] in a way where, for instance, the first level discusses only those subjects of natural science which are mentioned in that particular fairy tale. Even arithmetic has to submit to lessons of world view where only those calculations are to be performed which had been discussed beforehand and the exercises have to cover the same scope of notions and thoughts. This strict consistency resulted in the ridicule of the notion of concentration by the named pedagogues. Sometimes one has to really refrain from laughter when one sees how intelligent people are trying, in the sweat of their brow, to put everything into one bag. Concentration in this sense is really not to be recommended" (Ibid., 290).

Nevertheless, Schreiner did not reject concentration altogether: "Therefore the idea of concentration is not at all to be rejected; newer pedagogy has rightly set itself on this Herbart's idea but does not understand it in its broader sense as the afore mentioned pedagogues; it limits it somewhat as not to make the same focus for all subjects but to concentrate only those which have similar contents" (Ibid.).

Here followed Schreiner's description of formal steps "and this thought has the most value to be considered, namely that every curricular unit goes through five formal steps…." (Ibid.). After a short summary of psychological grounds of formal steps and an example Schreiner concluded: "We have to add that it is not necessary and sometimes not possible to perform each curricular unit exactly in five steps. Who would want to, would have to often push themselves and sometimes stretch the lessons without need because of theory. This would be formalism. But it would be useful without doubt if the teacher had formal steps in mind always when they are preparing for lessons. If one or the other does not fit them in some way, let them leave those out" (Ibid., 292).

At the end of the lecture, Schreiner briefly describes how the pedagogy of the day strives to make the lessons psychological. Before this, he pointed out that he did not entirely explain the teachings of formal steps in his short lecture. "I wanted only to inform those who probably had not occupied themselves with this question before" (Ibid.). We can see that it was not before the beginning of the 1890s when the formal steps (and at the same time, the entire Herbartianist pedagogic concept) became a topic of broader professional discussion, and that its initiator was actually Schreiner[31]. On the other hand, at least in professional debates, Herbartianism did not establish itself in its most orthodox (Ziller's and Rein's) version due to Schreiner's efforts.

In the following years, the teachings of the formal steps were established as an essential methodical improvement, which L. Černej (1894) connected with the demand that lessons should develop learners' independence; here he recommended Ziller's idea of formal steps. Although authors were explaining individual viewpoints on Herbartianism and critically evaluating them from the 1890s onwards, M. Lichtenwallner found it necessary to describe the basic characteristics of Herbartianist pedagogy as late as 1897. In his introduction, he points out that Herbart's followers triggered a large movement who also came across heavy resistance, which resulted in a hard struggle, leading to the creation of two pedagogic camps. He evaluated the situation in Slovenia as follows: "While the turbulent splashes of this movement on the pedagogic field woke up all northern teachers, while the burning question about Herbart's system was on the daily agenda there, we had a grave-like silence. Herbart-Ziller's movement was and still is for us mostly far away, somewhere in Turkey. Here and there individuals deal with this topic, seldom is this subject a part of the society's assemblies or official meetings" (Ibid., 132). Due to the lack of knowledge about Herbartianism in Slovenia, Lichtenwalner greeted the idea of a permanent committee of teachers in the Maribor region with approval in order to put the issue of theformal steps up for debate during the agenda of the last teacher conference, "the idea which is considered by Herbartians to be the basis of their aspirations" (Ibid.).

Lictenwallner's text was the first complete representation of the teachings of formal steps in Slovenia because his presentation starts with the explanation of the basics of Herbart's pedagogic and psychological concepts and then moves to an explanation of Ziller's conception. He states his opinion regarding formal steps only at the end of the article and presents the basis of the Herbartianist defence of formal steps in a very concise manner: "Here and there it was attempted to blame the formal steps that they are nothing more than an annoying template which takes from the teachers the necessary freedom during lessons. That is right, freedom of

31 We say »actually«, because the established image of Schreiner as a leading pedagogic authority of the period does not match the image of Schreiner as Herbartian.

activity is necessary for teachers in school! Nevertheless, they can never cope well without formal steps. Those who teach conscientiously, work with formal steps anyway - unintentionally, instinctively. Does it fit an educated person to regulate their doings and non-doings only by instinct...and not with safe steps towards goals which they strive for, goals, which they have to achieve? We can argue that a teacher who observes strictly defined principles in their work is higher ranked than the one who is guided only by, howbeit sometimes even the desired goal, only mysterious powers of their feelings. And laws on which the formal steps are founded? They are nothing else than that eternal road from the general to the specific, from concrete object to abstract thought, i.e. the inductive method...The 'template' of formal steps is thus in reality priceless. Under these instructions the teacher can build lesson plans in the easiest and fastest manner possible. The formal steps help them gather the material and also force them to arrange this material in a way which is best for child perception. Once started on this path, one will gladly teach with the help of formal steps and will certainly never leave this smooth path" (Ibid., 176).

In conclusion, Lichtenwallner appealed to those teachers enthusiastic about formal steps (and this was also the purpose of his article) to start publishing lesson plans made in accordance with formal steps. This appeal did not go unattended. In the same year, we can find a lesson plan with the title *Cyril and Methodius* in the central Slovene professional journal *Popotnik.* Its subtitle underscores the fact that it is a lesson plan made in accordance with formal steps (Lesjak 1897). The author (D. Lesjak) wrote in the introduction that he was very enthusiastic about teaching with formal steps because his work is made easier and that Lictenwallner's article helped him with it. In the following years, we can find numerous lesson plans devised in accordance with formal steps in both *Popotnik* and *Slovenski učitelj.* Their number reached their peak at the turn of the century, dropping off to almost zero after 1905. This decline can be attributed to the saturation of pedagogic literature with lesson plans, supported by the Slovene textbook publishing company *Slovenska šolska matica* (the president of whom was Schreiner), which in 1900 started publishing lesson plans for reading materials. At the same time, supervisors started publishing collections of lesson plans in the first years of the new century, which were prepared by teachers at official and social gatherings. The decline of interest in formal steps in pedagogic publications can also be attributed to the dispute between F. Hubad and V. Bežek, but these events belong to the next phase of the establishment of Herbartianism in Slovenia, which will be discussed later.

In individual parts of Slovenia, the establishment of Herbartianism in school practise, which was mostly associated with formal steps, took place irregularly and in a number of different ways. This establishment, along with the education of future teachers, occurred mostly on the part of teacher societies and official professional teacher conferences guided by school supervisors–who were often also teachers at teacher training colleges. As far it is possible to see from reports published by teacher conferences in the Austrian Littoral (Primorska region) (in the period between 1893-1901) formal steps or other Herbartianist topics were never discussed. We can also assume that those teacher training colleges did not pay more attention to formal steps than Lindner's textbook and that this was the reason why they were not present in school practise. In the region of Carniola (Kranjska) we can find only one (official) teacher report, which, although published in 1892, fits into the mentioned period. It is a conference of teachers from the district of Krško led by the county school supervisor F. Gaberšek. At the end of his lecture on five methodological (formal) steps, which were, as stated by the writer, presented "very thoroughly and extensively" he advises the ones present as follows: "[E]very teacher should go by these methodological steps and ensure themselves certain success in all subjects of public school" (Iz krškega okraja 1892, 253). The extent of the presence of formal steps in Ljubljana's teacher training colleges (in the region of today's capital of Slovenia) cannot be precisely defined. We can assume that it was at least a bit stronger than in the region of Austrian Littoral (Primorska), especially considering that at the time, the headmaster of the male teacher training college was F. Hubad. Formal steps in schools in the Carniola (Kranjska) region were probably barely used, if at all.

In the Lower Styria (Štajerska) region, the situation was completely different. At teacher conferences discussion of formal steps was not especially common, but was comparably greater than in other parts of Slovenia. Schreiner and his co-workers from the Teacher Training College in Maribor presented formal steps to teachers without officially forcing them and tried to raise enthusiasm. The writer from the conference of the Maribor teacher association wrote with enthusiasm in 1896 that "the eager and at the same time skilful teacher Mr. Jožef Fistravec performed...for the ones present instead of a lecture a lesson plan from geography in the workbook for the third grade. A good lesson plan is of greater effect in promoting teaching skills than a good theoretical lecture on the same subject... We noticed the formal steps in this lesson" (Maribor 1896, 347). In the same year, Schreiner, as district school supervisor, led a lecture at a country school in Dobravci. The teacher there who performed the lecture did well according to the writer: "The learners were interested in the topic and, for this reason, answered questions happily. If some of the listeners had not worked with formal steps before, they were certainly able to see their great importance at this lecture" (Iz mariborske okolice 1896, 220). To establish formal steps in school practise at schools in Lower Styria (Štajerska) it was an even more important fact that the encouragement came also from the ranks of teachers there. Here Lichtenwallner stood out; he lectured to the teacher society in Maribor the same year he published the above-mentioned article. The writer describes the lecture as follows: "Mr. M. Lichtenwallner lectures on the presented lecture (Darstellungsunterricht). The lecturer enthuses the listeners with his interesting, informative and concise speech about lessons concerning formal steps and the performed lessons. The president thanks the lecturer for a pleasant delight which is followed by loud approval" (Maribor, 1897, 110).

All this demonstrates that Lower Styria (Štajerska) saw the initiation of formal steps spontaneously, without pressure, by gradually training and exciting teacher practitioners. The initiation of modern teaching practises took place in the same manner, which is clearly illustrated by Lichtenwallner's professional bibliography (from the period after the First World War), he is best known in Slovene pedagogy as the representative of the working school, i.e. reform/progressive pedagogy, a pedagogic school of thought most criticised by Herbartianism. Although Lower Styria (Štajerska) was a centre of Herbartianism in Slovenia, nobody there identified with it. There was always a certain distance or association with the opponents of Herbartianism, who constantly reminded that formal steps cannot be carried out as a "template", i.e. mechanically, dogmatically, etc[32].

Because the presence of Herbartianism in Slovenia has been underexamined, the mere mention of formal steps is associated with the question "*Which formal step are you at now?*", a question supposedly posed by the supervisor when entering unannounced into the classroom. This question s demonstrates the rigidity and mechanic nature of the use of formal steps in classes where teachers were forced to perform a lesson exactly as designed in the lesson plan. It was this practise that first encouraged V. Bežek to start writing critical articles on formal steps, which led to the dispute with F. Hubad (Bežek 1903, 1903a, 1903b, 1904; Hubad 1903, 1903a). This activity belongs to the third period of initiation of Herbartianism, which started in 1901 when Hubad became territorial school supervisor for public schools in Carniola (Kranjska).

32 Here we can get the impression that this kind of use of formal steps was demanded by Ziller's stream of Herbartianism. This impression is mostly correct but the representatives of this stream decisively refuted the accusation that the theory of formal steps restricts teacher's freedom and mechanises their work and stressed the fact that the published lesson plans present only assistance for independent structuring of lessons (cf. Rein, Pickel, Scheller 1878/1903, 153-157).

## 3.4. The Period Between 1901 and 1914

With Hubad's now supervising the primary school system in Carniola (before this he was the headmaster of the Teacher Training College in Ljubljana), a thorough school reform began in this region. He accepted the work with the determination and sought to raise the level of individual classes and the whole school system, which was not as well developed as in Lower Styria (Štajerska). The official outcome of these efforts was a series of school orders (Ukazi in odredbe šolskih oblastev 1902), which were issued by the Carniola (Kranjska) territorial school board in May 1902. The order from 26 May 1902 applied to the rules at the beginning of lessons and determined free days. Among other things, these school orders determined that lessons must not be cancelled on account of processions, local church, secular holidays, or big fairs (Ibid., 170). A better use of school days was also the goal of the next order from 26 May 1902, which determined that school days cancelled due to contagious disease have to be made up during school holidays (Ibid., 185). Most interesting to our discussion is the order from 31 May 1902, which applied to the execution of teacher conferences, the preparation of teachers for class and teaching methods.

The territorial school board based this order by referencing existing state school legislation and can be understood as an effort towards a more thorough implementation of school regulations and their consolidation; most of all this was a unification of content and execution of classes and a strengthening of control.

The order contained the following decrees:

a) Teacher conferences do not have to include the communication of decrees *in extenso* because school managements also receive them and have to inform the teachers. The role of the supervisor is to explain those decrees at the conference needing explanation.

b) Teacher conferences should feature debates mainly about methodical issues and teaching observations. The topic should be discussed by all participants in written form. The methodical topics also have to feature lesson plans which must be evaluated by the district school supervisor, who also has to write a report on the conference and send it to the territorial school board. The clerks are appointed by the district school supervisor on the grounds of the material directly before the conference.

c) Each member of the conference has to thoroughly state the works used in their material.

d) The district school supervisor, i.e. a permanent committee, has to intentionally choose and divide the topics. Their number cannot be increased in the interest of thoroughness.

e) The teachers have to have enough time to prepare individual topics. (Ibid.)

“According to the importance of the thorough preparation of teachers for lessons and mastering (from science to practise) of renowned methods accepted by the county school conference”the order mentioned (Ibid., 171) also decreed that teachers have to thoroughly abide by this article, referring to § 62 of the School Regulations[33]. Teachers must “thoroughly prepare for lessons, divide the content of the lessons of the class they will teach into quarters, months and weeks before the start of the school year and note in their diary the activities and exercises they mean to do on individual days i.e. individual lessons” (Ibid.).

At the end of the order, the district school board received directions to execute the revision of the general curriculum (ordered one year before) in a manner which would enable the territorial school conference of 1903 to conclusively confirm it (Ibid).

This decree was substantially aided by the initiation of formal steps in Carniola (Krajnska) and virtually enacts them, although they were not mentioned. Regarding science and practise, it may be that the accepted and approved method was passed by the district school conference, but here the school supervisors had a decisive word (cf. Peček 1996). We can imagine that Hubad as territorial school supervisor recommended formal steps (he was probably encouraged by Schreiner) to district school supervisors and thus generated an additional intensive, intentionally guided training of teachers and the initiation of formal steps in lessons.

From 1902 to 1905, there was no official teacher conference in Carniola (Kranjska) where formal steps were not discussed. During this time, formal steps were also discussed by all teacher societies. These discussions became less frequent only after 1905, and after 1908, the topic completely disappeared from the programmes of teacher conferences and societies.

The comparison with Lower Styria (Štajerska) and Austrian Littoral (Primorska) shows that formal steps there were discussed less frequently. Furthermore, in Austrian Littoral (Primorska), such discussions were met with critical distance from the beginning, which can be attributed to Bežek’s critique. As headmaster of the Goriza (Gorica) teacher training college, he represented a certain expert authority, which also influenced the opinions of the supervisors of Austrian Littoral (Primorska).

---

33 This article decreed that individual subjects “should not be without mutual links but have to be understood as a unified educational material”. It also defined that no primary school subject has a defined teaching method but that the district and territorial school boards must work to prevent experimentation with methods: “The teachers have to master the methods acknowledged by science and practise and accepted by the district school conference.” (Schul- und Unterrichtsordnung für die allgemeinen Volksschulen 1870, 62).

Bežek was very contradictory in this dispute. In opposition to formal steps, he defended so called development-depiction lessons, a concept developed within Herbartianism, partially in opposition as a supplementation of Ziller's and Rein's concept. Instead of a five-stage division of lessons, he stood for Willmanns[34] three-stage division. The teacher's storytelling would be accompanied by the gradual formation of a story during discussion with students. In essence, Bežek's text represented a sharp critique of dogmatic use of formal steps in Carniola (Kranjska). The contradiction in Bežek's pursuance was mostly that despite the critique of Herbartianism (on a theoretical level) he stayed in the scope of Herbartianst paradigm. In striving to exceed formal steps he did not develop anything that would not be defended by some Herbartians. Nevertheless, Bežek cannot be labelled as a Herbartian. His text proves that he is coming closer to ideas of art pedagogy, which appeared in his work more as indefinite hunches–far from a conscious theoretical basis.

Hubad, who felt himself to be challenged expertly and work-wise and who built his answers upon an extraordinary knowledge of all aspects of Herbartianist theory, had no difficulty in convincingly refuting Bežek's ideas and consistently defending the formal steps, especially because he distanced himself from a dogmatic dependence on Ziller's line of Herbartianism. In all texts in Slovenia which dealt with the formal steps, we can find emphasis on the fact that they cannot be understood as a scheme which should be used by teachers in every lesson and that they should only be support for the teacher's independence of structuring the lessons. This view was also strongly defended by Hubad who, while citing Rein, stressed that the opposition towards formal steps comes mostly from not knowing them. People from Carniola (Kranjska) and Styria (Štajerska) were making up formal steps just like Schreiner. As they are taught at teacher training colleges (in Maribor and Ljubljana), a more thorough division of lessons is easier for teachers, but that "a template per-se…does damage anywhere, be it so or so many steps; this was emphasised always and everywhere" (Hubad 1903, 133). Apart from this, Hubad deservedly established that Bežek opposed the promotion of teacher independence in shaping lessons: "As far as 'freedom of method' is concerned, the critic is opposing himself because he beats down this freedom at the same time as he talks about it" (Ibid.). Bežek namely blamed the supporters of formal steps from Carniola (Kranjska) for being formalists who emphasise that five formal steps are a logical derivation of the apperceptional *process*. If on the other hand,

34 Although Willmann developed a reasonably independent pedagogic concept, Herbartians considered him as part of their circle.

we admit that we can convert and adjust the formal steps, "then the abstraction of five stages from the apperception process is not that logical[.]" (Bežek 1903a, 99) and summed up: "…I was for the idea to formulate a teaching articulation from the apperception process which would be strictly logical, for which no one could say that, because of circumstances or individual arbitrariness, one could stress one or the other part less or even leave it out; on the contrary, it would be so logically transparent that everybody should know and acknowledge it, that every teacher should execute it in every teaching process" (Ibid.).

The dispute raised attention and although Hubad had deeper theoretical arguments, most of the teachers in Slovenia were on Bežek's side. In his speech, they identified promotion of greater teacher autonomy, and a critique of violence, which was introduced simultaneously with the introduction of formal steps by district school supervisors. But of course, as thought by J. Bezjak, "…this dispute was educational and cleared the air and opinions about formal steps just like the storm clears the air" (1920, 236). After this polemic, we can find some firm critiques of the formal steps (e.g. Didaktični formalizem 1904; Demšar 1906), as well as some texts that still attribute them legitimacy, although with greater distance towards Herbartianism than was the case until that time. A greater emphasis on the fact that formal steps are only basic guidelines for teachers that can be adjusted according to the situation was also emphasised (e.g. Magerle 1904). One of the results of the polemic was also the first theoretical debate in printed form, written in a distinctively Herbartianist spirit by Schreiner (1903). With this book, Schreiner indirectly enters the polemic[35] and although he did not take sides, it is clear that he supported Hubad. In this book, he softens the critical distance towards Ziller he had displayed a couple of years before, and even defends him. In essence, this book is closest to Rein's pedagogic views, which were at that time still current and attention provoking. But as far as Schreiner's knowledge of modern

35 Schreiner had a true friendship with individuals on both sides of the polemic. Bežek also asked him to intervene to end the dispute, which did not work due to certain circumstances, especially Bežek's impatience. A detail from a letter where Schreiner explained his intervention to Bežek is especially interesting, as it illustrates the essence of the polemic: "In my judgement and, if I am not mistaking, you have also stated to me in person, your war is directed towards 'exaggeration' of formal steps. I presently do not have your essay at hand but cannot deny that my first impression was also that you are against formal steps in general. But this is not the question now. If one makes peace, one does not weigh words. Would you not submit an explanation? Maybe in a sense that you are fighting against those 'formalists' who ask: 'Which formal step are you at now?' etc. Maybe this dispute, which is definitely to our detriment, could end" (Bežek 1904, 2).

pedagogic currents goes, it is remarkable that he defended Herbartianism in such a pure form. With this text, Schreiner became the most conservative representative of Herbartianism in Slovenia.

The basic problem was not in the theory of formal steps, but in their use, which was dictated by school supervisors in Carniola (Kranjska). Bezjak, (as a contemporary) depicts a somewhat[36] reliable picture of these events: "Bežek acts as if it were claimed that formal steps were magnificent and the only correct choice. Here he is fundamentally wrong. Nobody argues that. Headmaster Schreiner introduced them as an important teacher tool in the teacher training college in Maribor who wrote a renowned analysis of the psychological horizon of the child and psychological process of teaching named *Analysis of the Psychological Horison of the Child and Psychological Process* about their essence and use the same year as the literary dispute between Bežek and Hubad began…The teachers used it to good effect, it was also very helpful to beginner teachers with their training. Because Schreiner was also a district school supervisor it is only natural he recommended them in his work. They thus also came to Kranjska where they were introduced by Hubad who was territorial [sic] school supervisor for state schools from 1901 to 1903 with the intention to bring order and justice into teaching practises which Hubad missed in his teaching observations. But if a district supervisor acted or demanded too fervently from the teachers to uphold formal steps exactly to the point, regardless if they did not know them well and thus were not able to prepare themselves in accordance to them even if they wanted to, this was not the fault of formal steps and they should not be taken the value and usefulness which was given to them by the excellent German pedagogues" (1920, 240).

An even more detailed description of the problems of introducing the formal steps in Kranjska is offered by E. Gangl (1903), who pointed out two aspects of Hubad's reform. Gangl wrote the following about what Bezjak referred to as excessively "fervent actions of supervisors": "Look! The so-called Hubad's period… was the start of the template spreading around our schools! The template came and clung our teachers' freedom into tight restraints. At the peak of it stand today as a new glistening planet on the school horizon formal steps which have been dissected for a long time and which have haunted our schools and befuddle our people. How would they not? They are not craftsmen to make a whole with the exactly tailored, filed and measured parts stacked without any positive value in eternal fear that a

36 We could say that he was biased in his interpretation of the dispute because Bežek also criticised him indirectly as a co-author of lesson plans. Nevertheless, the comparison with other sources indicates objectivity in Bezjak's writings.

‘formal stepper’ enters their school and asks: ‘Bei welcher formalen Stufe sind sie jezt?’ [which formal step are you at?] And if the poor devil does not know an answer immediately, he is sentenced to death: ‘Sie sind nicht vorbereitet [you are not prepared]!’ (Ibid., 217). With this, Gangl points out that the supervisors were the ones who interpreted the theory of formal steps in their own way, mainly as a tool that enabled complete control over the teachers. The school authorities thus were in the position to precisely plan every class, thereby stripping the teacher of all the autonomy. Herbartianist teachings about formal steps offered an ideal theoretical framework for this kind of practise, although Herbartians warned that this was a misuse of the teachings. How the misuse manifested itself in practise is explained by Gangl: “Formal steps and the so-called formulated sentences, the treasures of our lesson plans go nicely hand in hand. Formulated sentences are without doubt the high-end of modern methodology. If it is written: ‘A cat has a head, a body and limbs’, but the pupil says: ‘A cat has limbs, a body and a head’, someone can come and say with whole earnestness and strictness: ‘Your teaching methods are worthless - and therefore everything is worthless!” (Ibid., 217).

Another aspect pointed out by Gangl in connection with Hubad’s reform is connected to the material status of teachers: “The so-called Hubad period–let me be frank!–has brought about a completely false opinion in the leading circles, that it is enough if teachers daily get more and more work but we do not have to do anything to improve their material state” (Ibid., 210). This warning is still relevant today. Every reform performed by overworked and unsatisfied teachers is bound to fail because it inevitably provokes resistance. This also happened at that time. At the turn of the century, the issue of underpaid teachers became the central topic of union efforts and this did not improve until the First World War. In Lower Styria (Štajerska), teachers although largely unhappy with their conditions–were still better off, and many thus moved there from Carniola (Kranjska).

School system reform is especially inefficient if it does not also incorporate teachers’ knowledge and experience. In connection with this, Gangl wrote: “And our teachers are, because of constant stress, ill and nervous. You will hardly find a calm person among us. This wandering here and there, this bureaucracy which struts around in our schools, this horrible formalism which takes away our individuality and threatens to tailor all our lessons on one routine cannot have good consequences even though they are saying that these are the requirements of modern school. We have to remember that modern views are not a fruit of current mood, that it is not the only right thing which is imposed on us by higher authorities but that we also have to ask those for advice who have lower positions, but more experience” (Ibid., 210-211).

Gangl shows important details that summarize the circumstances that factored into implementing formal steps in Kranjska, along with their inappropriate use in class. Here Hubad played an important role, but to speak about a "Hubad period" would be misleading because Hubad was highly regarded and respected by most (especially liberally oriented teachers) and in addition, his reformist efforts and introduction of formal steps were seen as efforts to introduce a higher level of expertise into teaching. This period would be more accurately called the "Maier period".

In 1911, the *Učiteljski tovariš* issued several unsigned articles with the peculiar title *Maierejevci* (Maierians)[37]. That same year, and until 1914, a series of articles with similar content followed: This was an scholarly, personal and political critique of A. Maier–teacher at the practice teaching school at the male teacher training college in Ljubljana and supervisor of the Ljubljana district school. These articles are crucial in understanding the introduction and practise of formal steps in Carniola (Kranjska). They reveal that those notorious mechanicism, formalism, schematism and similar negative labels of Herbartianism were not so much due to the Herbartianist theory (which did help this perception), but mainly due to school practise, which was shaped by school supervisors and their particular demands. Furthermore, they show us that the strong resistance towards formal steps, initiated by Bežek in Carniola (Kranjska), can mainly be attributed to Maier because it was he who questioned teachers during supervisions which formal step they were currently at: "'[B]ei welcher Formalstufe sind sie jetzt?'–Maier was asking in schools! This, although unbelievable, is true!" (Maierjevci 1911, 1). This kind of resistance was not present in Lower Styria (Štajerska) or Austrian Littoral (Primorska). All evidence points to the fact that the school supervisors there understood formal steps less dogmatically–and therefore more correctly.

Because Maier's work will be discussed in detail in the last chapter, let us now sum up this presentation with a pithy quotation that best illustrates the fate of Herbartianism in Slovenia: "Maier knew only five formal steps from the whole pedagogic science, and these only by name. He did not know Herbart's ideas and still does not know them" (Ibid.).

## 3.5. Between Bureaucracy and Pedagogic Theory

It is possible to evaluate the presence of Herbartianism in Slovenia from different viewpoints. Its initiation into pedagogic theory is closely related to a higher scientific

---

37 First was Maierjevci (1911).

level of pedagogic discourse and the integration of the Slovenian pedagogic thought into actual pedagogic trends as well as reinforcing and raising professional confidence of teachers. First debates within Slovenia about Herbartianism also included critical evaluation, which enabled, on a theoretical level, to exceed the most disputable ideas. On the other hand, it is characteristic for the entire period under consideration that Herbartianism was never introduced as a complete, internally coherent pedagogic system that could enrich domestic pedagogic theory. In this sense, we can say that there was too little Herbartianism in Slovenia, considering the richness of Herbartianist theory in its discussion of pedagogy as a science, its philosophical examination of pedagogy, its insight into the relationship between the state and school, between theory and practise, etc. Instead of this, Herbartianist discussion was narrowed down to a discussion about formal steps (and their psychological basis), i.e. the methodology of lessons. This was helpful and resulted in higher quality lessons, but mostly in Lower Styria (Štajerska), where formal steps were introduced without constraint and where teachers could use them in accordance with their own professional judgement.

On the other hand, the initiation of formal steps in Carniola (Kranjska) was a different story and provides another perspective on Herbartianism in Slovenia. The teachings of formal steps has its flaws, but the negative image which follows these teachings until today has mainly been shaped by supervisors and is firmly connected to the bureaucratisation of pedagogy performed in Kranjska by school authorities. Formal steps in their hands turned into a means for state control over the execution of lessons and prevented teachers from performing their work autonomously.

# 4. The Education of Teachers in Slovenia and the Application of "Common Sense" Herbartianism[38]

The State Primary School Act [Reichsvolkschulgesetz] of 1869 can be considered the most important school act of the former Austro-Hungarian Monarchy. Many standards and systemic solutions of this Act had been a basis of school legislation for almost a century in countries which were a part of the Austro-Hungarian Empire. This is especially true for teacher training colleges, which with this law became the central institutions for training teachers and presented, in comparison to the former arrangement, a completely new and fundamentally higher quality educational experience. Pedagogic historiography offers them too little attention; researchers are generally more interested in the theoretical concepts inform these academic circles than the practical pedagogic execution of these concepts.

The entire area of present-day Slovenia was then a part of the Austro-Hungarian Monarchy and thus belonged to its jurisdiction. With the enforcement of the State Primary School Act, teacher training colleges began to be established here, but there were not many. Slovenia is small and has a small population–this was also one of the reasons why Slovenes in the Austro-Hungarian Monarchy could not assert many national interests, linguistic ones, among others. German was the more established language of instruction than Slovene at teacher training colleges in the territory populated by Slovenes, although these colleges also trained teachers for Slovene primary schools. The pressure of Germanisation was also the reason why the Slovenes did not manage to establish their own university until 1919 with the downfall of the Austro-Hungarian Empire.

Pedagogic thought originating at universities had a great influence on the school system in individual national environments of that time. This was nevertheless the time when teachers also greatly influenced the theory of education. Regular primary school teachers with a degree from a teacher training college were frequently among the writers of professional andscientific texts in the scholarly journals of the time. But the teaching profession was mostly developed by teachers at teacher training colleges who were, on the basis of their experience, experts on teaching

38 This chapter is an expanded and corrected version of an article first published in Italian (Protner 2012).

methodology for their own subjects. This also applied to the directors of teacher training colleges, who usually taught pedagogic subjects at their institutions (pedagogics, didactics, history of pedagogics); they led preparations for lectures, the execution, teaching observations and conferences where the analysis of the whole proceedings was run under their supervision. Whether pedagogic training of future teachers followed routine patterns with a lesson plan of prescribed content, or if this training was also a trial in establishing new pedagogic ideas, depended on the pedagogic skill and innovation of the directors. Between 1869 and the First World War, the Herbartianist pedagogic concept was predominant in teacher training; gradually, it became replaced by reformist (progressive) concepts from the end of the nineteenth century onwards. Amidst this turmoil in pedagogic concepts, it was largely the directors of teacher training colleges who added the most to the professional qualifications of teachers (shaped the pedagogic education of teachers with expert appearance).

## 4.1. Henrik Schreiner and the Teacher Training College at Maribor

The Teacher Training College at Maribor stood out during the time it was led by Director Henrik Schreiner (cf. Protner 2002a). The Austrian school authorities appointed Schreiner as Director in 1890 on the grounds of the professional reputation he gained as a teacher of natural science subjects at the Teacher Training College in Bolzano, where he was previously employed from 1878. His German-sounding surname was also a consideration, as it seemed to promise a person who could fortify the German character of the institution. In reality, Schreiner was a Slovene patriot who was able to ease national polarisation pressures during his management of the institution (1890–1920). He was able to adeptly reconcile the pressures of the Austrian official school authority on the one hand, and the growing Slovene national awareness on the other. As he was able to find the correct measure for establishing tolerant national coexistence at the institution he led, he was also able to choose various pedagogical concepts which were, under his supervision, introduced to future teachers.

Schreiner's management of the Teacher Training College at Maribor helps illustrate the state of teacher education at that time. This period of pedagogic history is not based on big stories, piercing theoretical ideas, extraordinary pedagogic innovations, but rather on moderation, common sense and an avoidance of extremes in both theory and practice. Schreiner's contemporaries knew to value this stance; they attributed him with a high degree of professional authority. This respect among pedagogues from the past and not-so-distant past is evident in a monumental memorial built to his memory at his Teacher Training College.

Most of the written sources about Schreiner (along with listing credits and pedagogic views) usually mention that Schreiner stood for the introduction of formal steps in primary school practise. The formal steps are one of the basic categories of Herbartianist pedagogy and Schreiner can undoubtedly be classified as one of the most important representatives of Herbartianism in Slovenia. This is why it is so much more interesting that many of Schreiner's biographies do not mention this theoretical stance at all, or it is only mentioned in connection with a kind of apology for this "delusion" of his, together with a warning that Schreiner did not accept the negative extremes of Herbartianism. Šilih (the leading didactic of the post-war era), for instance, wrote that "Schreiner's broadest pedagogic work 'Analysis of the Psychological Horison of the Child and Psychological Process; Teachings of formal steps' proves that its author was completely in the bonds of the official Austrian Herbartianist pedagogics. But the Herbartianist template disgusted him, as he himself warned against it" (1950, 667). Elsewhere he estimates that in the aforementioned work, Schreiner "represents himself as a follower of Herbartianist pedagogy but as a critical spirit who does not recap the teachings of the authorities blindly" (Šilih, 1951, 224). Šilih writes in such a way that Herbartianist label would be disgraceful. He was also not able to avoid the predominantly negative evaluation of Herbartianism imposed by reformist (progressive) pedagogy from the turn of the century onward in the struggle to establish a new pedagogic paradigm. Modern explanations of Herbartianist pedagogy do not allow such simplified evaluations. Herbartianism cannot simply be equated with Herbart's pedagogy, but more importantly, Herbartianism cannot be equated with the most radical theoretical ideas and practical derivations– Herbartianism is a fundamentally richer pedagogic movement that also established a strong internal opposition and critical (self) evaluation. This is why we can say that Schreiner was the most important representative of Herbartianist pedagogy in Slovenia and by saying this, we do not diminish his reputation at all (see Chapter 3.3). We can also say that Herbartianist theory informed most of the pedagogic activities he conducted as headmaster speaker at teacher assemblies, supervisor, writer of theoretical discussions and textbooks, and as the president of the publishing office *Slovenian School Society* [Slovenska šolska matica]. By understanding the extent of his influence, we can also explain the dimension of Herbartianism in Slovenia. Let us now look at Schreiner's contributions to each of the aforementioned fields.

### 4.1.1. Schreiner as the Headmaster of the Maribor Teacher Training College

Upon Schreiner's arrival to the Maribor teacher training college in 1890, there were already teacher training regulations in force, which were determined by the *State Primary School Act of 1869* [Reichsvolksschulgesetz 1869]. The institution which he took over was organised by the *Statute for Male and Female Teacher Training Colleges* [Organisationsstatut für Lehrerbildungsanstalten, 1874] and later, by the revised organisation statute [Organisationsstatut der Bildungsanstalten für Lehrer und Lehrerinnen an öffentlichen Volksschulen in Österreich, 1886][39]. This legislation was significantly (but not fully) shaped by Herbartians (as we have shown in Chapter 2.3) the concept of teacher education in Austria-Hungary was particularly strongly influenced by K.V. Stoy, who organised a seminar for the education of primary school teachers in Beilitz (Bielsko-Biała) in 1867. Stoy integrated a lot of experience and theoretical reasoning formed by German Herbartians (along with T. Ziller) during the management of university pedagogic seminars. Herbart's understanding of the relationship between theory and practise was at the forefront; this was organisationally improved by Herbartians in the model of mutual connection of three aspects of teacher education named Theoretikum, Praktikum and Kritikum. We can find almost all essential elements of Stoy's (and Ziller's) conception of the organisational execution of theoretical and practical training in the *Statute for Male and Female Teacher Training Colleges*[40]. This statute put forth the requirement of building a pedagogic thought circle (*Theoretikum*) among teacher candidates, meaning that they had to become acquainted with pedagogic theory and its related disciplines. It ran both before and during with the practical training period (*Praktikum*) and included teaching observations, along with practical teaching performances in the form of individual trials. During practical performances, the teacher candidate had to prepare a thorough lesson plan under the supervision of the teaching staff and the head teacher, who sees to the uniformity of didactic and pedagogic outlook of the workbook. After the teaching performance, there is a discussion and critique (*Kritikum*) of the candidate's performance. This model should promote the influence of pedagogic science (Herbartianist pedagogic theory and didactic base of classes) on teacher work. It is only the scientific basis, from which relatively thorough instructions for the teacher's concrete

39 This legislation was thoroughly presented and analysed by Gönner (1967) and Strmčnik (1970).

40 The revised organisation statute from 1886 did also not essentially change them.

functioning in class are derived, which should inform conscientious professional practise. Along with this, teacher training should contribute to the formation of the teacher's personality and their devotion to the profession.

Schreiner's reports on the Maribor Teacher Training College show that Herbartianism here (due to him) was more present than the school legislation demanded. The description of school practice in his first report (Schreiner 1892a) is in line with school regulations, but the students also had to write a weekly report of individual classes of practice teaching school, along with the teaching observations and presentations prescribed by the legislation. This way the teacher candidate could get acquainted with the way of conducting school administration; it is also important that the teacher candidates could orient themselves "before every practical presentation on the material which they had to implement on the basis of a copy of the weekly report which they had in hand" (Ibid., 66). This is a characteristic Herbartianist demand, the purpose of which is to ensure the continuation and harmonisation of work on the practice teaching school. This demand was further supported by Schreiner with the requirement that the student teachers cooperate in making school reports. Schreiner's demand (which was not prescribed by school legislation) was also characteristically Herbartianist, in the way that the student teachers were to write individual lesson plans of individual students of practice teaching school (Ibid.) in accordance with a set pattern, which should sharpen their ability of psychological child observation. All student teacher activities were linked with written documentation, which is also characteristic of Herbartianist doctrine (cf. Protner 2001).

Along with the organisational reform, Schreiner also introduced changes in curriculum at the practice teaching school, as well as the didactic and methodical layout of classes. Here he also had to consider school legislation, which was loose enough to allow for introducing some characteristic Herbartianist ideas into the practice teaching school (educational aspects of lessons, formal steps, concentration of lessons). We can recognise them in the second report from 1895, in which Schreiner comments on the introduction of student teachers into school practise: "[I]n essence of educational classes, firstly to strive for presenting every lesson unit as a closed entity. In the end, exemplary presentations which were conducted in teaching observations were executed in accordance with formal steps without becoming strictly formalist; the student teachers were instructed to make lesson plans along these lines. The 4th year student teachers were also instructed to make lesson plans for practise lessons in accordance with formal steps and execute them accordingly" (Ibid., 4). Schreiner devoted a lot of attention to the concentration of lessons. Individual lessons were not treated separately, but as parts of larger lesson units. Therefore third grade student teachers executed a larger lesson unit (as was permitted by the curriculum) under his supervision (in a successive line of practise lessons). First, they made an agreement about the plan of the envisioned lesson unit during the preparation conference, when they discussed "how to perform concentration of local studies...as well as natural sciences, history, language (essay!) and musical education" (Ibid.). As an introduction to the envisioned lesson unit, they used the free afternoon for a walk with third grade students, who were accompanied by fourth year students of the teacher training college under the supervision of the headmaster. During the walk, they performed the necessary observations and defined further observational tasks for the students. "This was accompanied by individual lectures which the student teachers listened to (when it was possible) during classes which were allocated on the timetable for lesson presentations and lesson trials. Conferences, which followed, featured new detailed discussions about mutual relationships of individual curricular units and their relation to the whole" (Ibid.).

Schreiner faced numerous problems during the introduction of Herbartianist ideas into the curriculum of the practice teaching school; he had to reconcile Herbartianist doctrine and the official curriculum. On the basis of clear theoretical grounding, he managed to coordinate the work of both the teachers at the teacher training college (who were mainly methodologists) and the teachers at the practice teaching school to encourage mutual cooperation as well as theoretical and practical improvement. The Maribor Teacher Training College became a centre of experimental trials of Herbartianist pedagogic theory in Slovenia under Schreiner's leadership.

## 4.1.2. Schreiner as a Speaker at Teacher Assemblies

At the time Schreiner was introducing Herbartianist practise to the Maribor Teacher Training College, he also founded and presented some new theoretical ideas to the broader circle of primary school teachers at the end of 1891. At that time, he lectured on the concentration of lessons for the *Maribor Teacher Society* (the meeting was held on the premises of the College). The meagre report from this lecture (H. 1891) suggests that it was meant to gain teachers' cooperation. The lecture was followed by a lively debate, which resulted in two conclusions:

"a) To work towards the goal where lessons in our schools are in due time constructed on the basis of concentration.

b) To create meaningful detailed syllabuses for all categories of schools of our district on the basis of local studies" (Ibid.). The task was supposed to be executed by the Society's board.

Shortly after, the text from this lecture was published in the journal *Popotnik* (Schreiner 1892). Along with a theoretical explanation of the concept of concentration, the text also displayed his tendency towards introducing formal steps. Before this, the theoretical foundation of formal steps was published by G. Majcen (1891), a teacher at the practice teaching school of the Maribor Teacher Training College, which further illustrates how expert professional activity at this institution flourished under Schreiner's leadership.

A decisive moment in introducing Herbartianism to Slovenia can be (as we have shown in the Chapter 3.3) attributed to Schreiner's lecture to the assembly of the *Union of Slovenian School Societies* in 1893. Afterwards, he succeeded in making some Herbartianist ideas part of the basis for further development of Slovene schools. In the introduction to *Newest Aspirations for Reformation on the Pedagogic Field*, Schreiner explains that he sees the purpose of the assembly as "coming together…only in main points of our operation, to establish the direction which we will face from here on[.]" (Peta štajerska učiteljska konferenca, 261). Schreiner obviously identified Herbartianism as the one modern reform not well known enough in Slovenia that should be introduced. He pointed out that he did not want to evaluate Herbart's ideas and that Herbart's psychology was already surpassed, but at the same time he pointed out: "…Herbart marks a new age in the history of didactics and pedagogy, an era we call scientific" (Ibid., 262). With this lecture, Schreiner obviously wanted to encourage reform in the Slovene primary school system, which should be based on another scientifically based, theoretical foundationwhich would enable Slovene schools to come into contact with foreign pedagogy. Among these novelties, Schreiner mainly thought of that what was already being introduced and tried at the teacher training college: Concentration of lessons and formal steps.

Pedagogically, Schreiner was extraordinarily proficient and familiar with the situation abroad– he was well acquainted with the polemics which arose from some of the most radical theoretic ideas among leading Herbartians (mainly T. Ziller). Along with a developed feeling for practical feasibility, he also pointed to some exaggerations parallel to the introduction of Herbartianism. He thus presented Ziller's idea of concentration with ridicule and at the same time strove for the introduction of a less radical form. Schreiner focused most on introducing formal steps. He briefly describes and psychologically grounds them in the aforementioned lecture as such: "We have to add that it is not necessary and sometimes not possible to perform each curricular unit exactly in five steps. Who would want to, would have to often push themselves and sometimes stretch the lessons without need because of theory. This would be formalism. But it would be useful without doubt if the teacher had formal steps in mind always when they are preparing for lessons. If one or the other does not fit them in some way, let them leave those out" (Ibid.). Schreiner also determined in this case the basic guidelines for the sensible and rational transfer of the theoretical basis into school practise. With the introduction of formal steps, he saw a means that would foster the support of the teachers for rational and expertly grounded articulation of a lesson. Furthermore, by making teachers aware of the critiquepositing that formal steps restrict teacher creativity and force them into mechanicism and schematism, he encouraged independence and expert deliberation among Slovene teachers.

Schreiner's initiative was effective. Due to his work, formal steps became the main topic of different teacher conferences and local gatherings in the years to follow, as well as a general didactic framework of school practise (first in Slovene Styria (Štajerska) and after 1901, in a more extensive part of Slovene territory). Schreiner's opinion was also relevant after the tumultuous polemic about formal steps had begun. This is a dispute (see Chapter 3.4) led by Viktor Bežek and Fran Hubad in the journal *Popotnik* in 1903 and 1904. The discrepancy was caused by Bežek's findings that there is more and more debate over formal steps in Carniola (Kranjska) that they are talked about as a modern field (Bežek 1903, 1), because they were allegedly already passé in the rest of the world. He also illustrated the formalism and schematism of the use of formal steps in school practise, describing how a county supervisor demands that teachers clearly answer the question "at which formal step they are currently", when he enters the class (Ibid., 33). Hubad, who as a territorial school supervisor strove to introduce formal steps in schools in Carniola (Kranjska), theoretically arguing their relevance and defending them in this polemic. Evidence suggests that this was encouraged by Schreiner.

Schreiner joined the polemic indirectly. Everything points to the fact that the expert community expected him to take sides regarding this issue. He obliged with a lecture organised by the *Slovenian School Society* in the National Hall in Ljubljana. Here he again took a stand for expert, deliberate and autonomous use of formal steps. The timely relevance of this issue is confirmed by the attendance at the lecture; there were so many participants that some of them had to stand in the foyer. The reporter wrote the following about Schreiner's lecture and the response to it: "In general [Schreiner] is for executing classes in accordance with defined steps but he thinks that it is neither appropriate nor beneficial to divide every lesson into exactly five steps because this would lead the teachers to boring formalism! Many times one or the other step has to be cancelled; in some subjects complying with formal steps is even impossible. During the speech and especially at the end of the talk the listeners agreed with the lecturer loudly and with passionate applaud "(Predavanje v "Slovenski Šolski Matici", 1903, 95).

During the entire time, Schreiner was trying to calm those on both sides of the dispute. He maintained friendly relations with both but he was obviously more theoretically inclined towards Hubad. This can also be seen from his book *Analysis of the Psychological Horizon of the Child and the Psychological Process of Learning* with the subtitle *Teachings about Formal Steps* (Schreiner 1903) which was published on the request of the *Slovene School Society* committee to calm the passionate debate by him as an authority. Formal steps were never imposed by Schreiner, although he defends them in the aforementioned book. A deeper meaning has to be attributed to his wish "not to have a member of Slovene teachers who would not be well acquainted with the theory of formal steps from this time on, regardless their opinion about them. Because a really firm scientific basis enables the teacher to have a deliberate, independent judgement, it raises the teacher-craftsman into the teacher-artist" (Schreiner 1903, 4). Together with Herbartianism, Schreiner brought the Slovene environment a new understanding of the professional character of a teacher and strengthened the belief that broad reaching pedagogic and theoretical skill is the basis of school practise.

### 4.1.3. Schreiner as School Supervisor

Schreiner became the district school supervisor for the Maribor district in 1892 and held this position until 1899. His work there is illustrated by J. Bezjak (somewhat biasedly but realistically enough). He wrote: "This was the biggest gain for teachers of this district; because Schreiner carried his educational knowledge and his didactic and methodological views among his teachers and informed them with new ideas which sprung up on the educational field. He performed his supervisions in home teacher conferences he held every year in every school as well as with county school assemblies where he taught teachers and enthused them with progress in teaching methods and one's own education" (Bezjak 1921, 252).

At his first official teacher conference in the Maribor district (H. 1891) as district school supervisor, Schreiner advised teachers to introduce written preparations and announced he would look them over during his next supervisions. This shows that he started a new, formerly unknown practise, which would fundamentally help to introduce the formal steps. While the report does not mention formal steps, they were likely discussed at this conference because the teachers in Maribor and the surroundings were probably acquainted with Majcen's discussion, which announced a new direction in the methodological execution of classes. Schreier strengthened his influence on teachers in Maribor as he and Majcen intensively joined the *Teacher Society for the Maribor District*. We have already mentioned that he held a lecture on lesson concentration at the end of 1891, and shortly after the members of the society elected him as president (Maribor 1892).

Schreiner overcome local borders with this lecture at the fifth assembly of the *Union*, which can be considered a milestone in the process of introducing Herbartianism in Slovenia. But although the assembly took place before the forum, which combined all Slovene teachers, Herbartianism was not introduced evenly in all parts of the country. Herbartianism was strongest in Lower Styria (Štajerska) because of Schreiner. Reports about official and social assemblies in Kranjska and Primorska regions do not mention discussions on Herbartianist topics until the turn of the century.

Discussion of formal steps at teacher conferences in Lower Styria (Štajerska) were not especially common, but their presence was incomparably greater than in other parts of Slovenia. Here in particular we have to point out that Schreiner and his coworkers presented formal steps to teachers without forcing them and tried to encourage their enthusiasm. This is apparent in numerous reports on the activities of the *Teacher Society for the Maribor district* during Schreiner's leadership. The author wrote with enthusiasm in 1896 that "the eager and at the same time skilful teacher Mr. Jožef Fistravec performed…for the ones present instead of a lecture a lesson plan from geography in the workbook for the third grade. A good lesson plan is of greater effect in promoting teaching skills than a good theoretical lecture on the samesubject…We noticed the formal steps in this lesson" (Maribor 1896). In the same year, Schreiner lead a teaching observation at a country school in Dobravci. Gselman, the teacher there who performed the lecture, did well according to the writer: "The learners were interested in the topic and, for this reason, answered questions happily. If some listeners had not worked with formal steps before they definitely saw their great importance on this occasion" (Iz mariborske okolice 1896, 220). That year, teaching observations led by Schreiner became a regular form of additional teacher training in the scope of the Society and shows that they were well received by the teachers. These lectures did not force the formal steps, but served as a form of professional training in which teachers did did not only participate in carrying out orders, but also acted as co-designers of expert solutions. Schreiner succeeded in creating a friendly and simulative collegial atmosphere. The reporter mentions that teaching observation was a chance for the teachers "to state their opinion and views about the lesson plan. There was broad satisfaction. Mr. Giselman can be proud that he was expressed full acknowledgement also by the supervisor…After a lively, insightful talk almost all of us headed towards Slivnica. The sun was beating down, we were swimming in sweat, so to say, but we were, without exception, all content and in good mood. We realised with delight that we learned something" (Ibid.).

The reporter was equally enthusiastic about the next teacher observation (M. C., 1896a) where the lesson plan was carried out at a school in Ruše by Lichtenwalner: "The lesson was especially interesting because it was carried out exactly according to formal steps. The attendees were well informed about their use as if they had read a whole book about them. This is why teacher observations are so valuable, we cannot overestimate them; of course they have to last several hours. I am tempted to write more on formal steps bit will leave it at that because this issue will be raised at this year's official conference and because I know that the discussion will also be published in the journal 'Popotnik'…I claim that who knows their essence and shapes their lessons in accordance with them achieves much more. This is the only way of teaching thoroughly and interestingly. If lessons do not have these marks, they are not educational. Mr. Lichtenwallner taught, as stated before, strictly in accordance with formal steps and hale Pohorje dwellers talked, answered and corrected so earnestly that the listener's heart was full of joy" (Ibid., 259). Unfortunately, we were unable to find the report from the official teacher conference for the Maribor district where, as stated by the reporter, formal steps were discussed. 1896 can definitely be evaluated as a year when formal steps began to be intentionally introduced into schools in Lower Styria (Štajerska).

The enthusiastic report of the sixth and seventh teacher observation at the Maribor district (C. 1897) call for teachers to organise in other districts: "It is already being copied in some places. Long live the idea and its father Mr. supervisor Schreiner" (Ibid., 286). Reports on these teaching observations usually state that individual presentations were followed by a discussion. The report on the eighth teacher observation is most eloquent (Mi-ci, 1898) and clearly shows how the introduction of formal steps also presented the Herbartianist triad of complementing theory with the critique of the practise. The reporter wrote on this subject: "The debate after the class was finished so lively as none before. I felt as if we all wanted to become supervisors. This was quite a scuffle! But I have to admit that I did not find any passion here…Mr. Supervisor always gave the first word to attendees and only then expressed his opinion. The referent was always given an opportunity to defend themselves if this was necessary" (Ibid.). Although the final word always belonged to the leader (as in Herbartianist university pedagogic seminars), the teachers were not passive receivers, but played an active role. This was very important for raising their self-confidence and their professional status as teachers.

When Hubad became territorial school supervisor in Carniola (Kranjska) in 1901, he tried to reform the local school system according to Schreiner's model. The fate of his reformist efforts is also informative for today's planners of school reforms. As formal steps were introduced without coercion, professionally thought over and with the support of teachers in Lower Styria (Štajerska) under Schreiner's leadership, Carniola (Kranjska) experienced bureaucratic constraint, which inhibited teachers' professional autonomy. Another aggrevating circumstance was that the reform coincided with a general economic recession and reduction in school funding. The biggest damage was dealt to his (well meaning) reformist efforts by A. Maier, the district supervisor for city schools in Ljubljana, who launched a general resistance among teachers with his forceful, unprofessional and bureaucratically limited activity (more on this in Chapter 6). A contemporary wrote: "Before him, there is fear, horror, shivering - after him despair, tears, clatter with teeth, brandishing closely clenched fists! He bewildered teachers of two districts with his cruelty and ignorance; he discredited the whole country with his formal steps. Confusion was complete!" (Maierjevci 1911, 1). It was Maier who asked teachers 'Which formal step are you at' upon entering the classroom and it was his doing that rendered the *formal steps* (and Herbartianism) as "old school". As supervisor, Schreiner was received in a completely different manner and teachers in lower Styria (Štajerska) had an entirely different attitude towards formal steps. Schmoranzer, for instance, wrote that "the cheeks of students shone with happiness when Schreiner stepped into the school...This is why we will not be amazed that the teachers also were happy when Schreiner came to supervise. This I have been told many times by numerous teachers of the Maribor district" (Schmoranzer 1920, 20)

There is no doubt that Schreiner's personal qualities helped him gain the influence and authority he enjoyed among teachers and the expert community. Schreiner did, however, have a clear vision for the development of the Slovene primary school system from the beginning based on a deliberate and coherent theoretical basis. The dimension of Schreiner's influence is rounded out by his publishing activities.

### 4.1.4. Schreiner as a Textbook Author and President of the Publishing Company of the Slovenian School Society

Schreiner, apart from promoting the introduction of formal steps (and concentration of lessons) also campaigned for the reform of primary school readers from 1892[41]. Texts with realistic content, which were until that time an integral part of primary school readers, should be replaced with belles lettres. This idea also had a decidedly Herbartianist origin–together with other reformist interventions, these readers

41 He spoke about this on the 5th Štajerska teacher conference (Peta štajerska /.../, 1892).

would contribute to a better educational value of lessons (cf. Protner 1999a, 2010). The next step towards the realisation of this idea was in form of *Memorandum of the Union of Slovenian Teacher Societies Regarding the Reform of Folk School Readers* (*Spomenica...*, 1895) from *1895*, which was addressed to the Ministry for Education by the *Union*. This important document shows that Slovene pedagogy (mostly because of Schreiner) was then developed enough for a self-sustaining and independent formation of primary school. The proposed reform of primary school readers was taken up in 1897 by J. Koprivnik and G. Majcen who published the book *Introduction for Slovene Folk Schools*; it was supplemented by Hubad and Schreiner in 1902 with the *Reader for General Folk Schools*. But the dimension of this project gains a whole new meaning when considered together with the activity of the publishing house Slovenian School Society [Slovenska šolska matica], which was presided over by Schreiner from its founding in 1900 until his death in 1920. A review of books published by the Slovene School Society during this period (Seznam knjig..., 1940) reveals that Schreiner's editorial policy was almost entirely in tune with the Herbartianist ideals he introduced to Slovene teachers.

Because both textbooks mentioned no longer had realistic content, the resulting gap was filled by the *Slovene School Society*– it started publishing books meant to help teachers in history and natural sciences (before being integrated into readers, content was meant to be thoroughly communicated by teachers). The first volume of the *Slovenian School Society* features Apih's historical subject matter for folk schools *History Learning Material for Folk Schools* (first collection)–from 1906 on, five more collections were issued. From 1909 to 1911, L. Pivko published three collections of the *History of the Slovenians*. We can also place E. Kukovič book, *Local Studies in Folk Schools*, from 1912 in this collection.

Natural science content was systematically integrated by the Slovenian School Society from 1905 onwards. Until the First World War, the publisher issued five more titles in this field. When Majcen issued the first collection of *The Sense Perception Teachings for the 1st School Year*, it was followed by a second collection the following year. In 1907, L. Černej, B. Stupica and L. Schreiner published *The Sense Perception Teachings for the 2nd and 3rd School Year* (2nd collection); a collection with the same title was issued the following year by F. Gabršek, J. Dimnik and J. Heric. The same authors published the third collection in 1909.

This content was also introduced into lesson plans, which showed an exemplary methodical execution of individual lessons with the use of texts from primary school readers. In 1902, the first part of *The Lesson Plans for Folk School Readers* was published. In 1903, the first collection of the second part of lesson plans with folk readers *The Lesson Plans for Folk School Readers* was published, followed by the second collection in 1904, and the third collection in 1905. These readers were connected with the aforementioned Schreiner-Hubad's *Readers for General Folk Schools* as well as Josin-Gangl's *2nd reader* (this reader had realistic content). It was these lesson plans that finally established a Herbartianist outline of classes in Slovene schools because they were generally based on the theory of formal steps. Schreiner further established and explained this theory in the (aforementioned) *Analysis of the Psychological Horizon of the child and the Psychological process of Learning*, which was published by the *Slovenian School Society* in 1903. Apart from this, the Slovenian School Society intentionally published methodicals for individual subjects, which were, content-wise, in tune with Schreiner's publishing policy. A thorough theoretical argumentation of the reform of primary school readers (in the described sense) was presented in the first year of the *Slovenian School Society* by F. Ilešič in his book *On the Teaching of Slovenian Language*. Herbartianist influences can also be seen in the book by J. Bizjak, *Special Didactics of Slovene Teaching Language in Folk Schools* (1st collection, 1906, 2nd collection, 1907) and F. Hauptmann's *Special Didactics of Natural History*. It is harder to confirm the influence of Herbartianism in Druzovič's *Special didactics of singing in folk schools* (1906) and Lavtar's *Special Didactics of Arithmetic in Folk Schools* (1909, 1910, 1911, 1913), but this does not change the fact that Schreiner was systematically introducing Herbartianist pedagogy through his editorial policy.

A certain deviation from this pedagogy is observed in M. Lichtenwallner's book *Free Essays in Folk School* (1908 1st collection, 1909 2nd collection), which already announced the penetration of reformist (progressive) pedagogy and both of Bežek's books: *General Didactics with Introduction Into Psychology* (1913 1st volume, 1914, 2nd volume, 1915 3rd volume) and *General Didactics with Introduction Into the Logic* (1916 – 1918 1st volume, 1919 2nd volume), which were more related to art pedagogy than Herbartianism. Schreiner carefully followed pedagogic innovations in Europe and at home. He was a contemporary of the irrevocable pluralisation of pedagogic theory which pushed out Herbartianism as the dominant pedagogic paradigm from the end of the nineteenth century onwards; Schreiner joined this movement as a tolerant professional which can be seen also by his editorial relationship towards the mentioned books.

## 4.2. Herbartianism and Pedagogic Standards

Today it is hard to imagine that an individual could possess the kind of powerful, national influence on school practise as Schreiner did during his time. As the schoolmaster of the Maribor Teacher Training College, he developed and defended the chosen Herbartianist theoretical pedagogic concept and established it among his coworkers and future teachers (students). As the president of the teacher society, he presented this concept (with the help of his colleagues) to the teachers of his school district. As their school supervisor, he further explained this concept and monitored whether it was being suitably executed in school practise. His work thus helped define the direction of the reformist aspirations of Slovene primary school at that time. He followed this aspiration theoretically and organisationally; he finally reinforced this aspiration through his publishing activities at the *Slovenian School Society*, which indirectly contributed to the content and outlay of classes with manuals (and other literature) before World War I and also during both wars.

His personal strength certainly contributed to this, but the decisive influence can probably be attributed to the professional and argumentative convincingness he gained from referencing the scientific systematics of Herbartianist pedagogy. The question remains whether Schreiner would label himself as a representative of Herbartianist pedagogyhis first articles were critiques of some of the leading Herbartianist pedagogues and he rejected many things completely. He also did not discuss many central themes of Herbartianism. But we do not identify Herbartianism in Schreiner's pedagogy only through the presence of characteristic Herbartianist topics (formal steps, concentration, educational aspect of classes, perceptions as the basis for forming the psyche), but also (or mainly) in relation towards pedagogy as science. Schreiner's arrival marked the introduction of new, higher standards of discussion and writing about pedagogic issues in Slovenia. Thus, it is necessary to redefine and point out the positive role of Herbartianism, together with Schreiner, in the development of Slovene education.

# 5. The Attitude of Catholic Pedagogues Towards Herbartianist Pedagogy in Slovenia[42]

Adl-Amini, Oelkers and Neuman list the political context as one of the reasons for the dominance of Herbartianism in the second half of the nineteenth century:

"Herbart's pedagogy emerged as the leading paradigm in a noticeable parallel with the decline of the liberal bourgeoisie in Germany after 1848. Ziller's protestant scientism was basically better adjusted to political-pedagogical self-understanding of the pro-revolutionary period as, for instance, Diesterweg's anti-clerical, natural-scientific education and school. Although the history of political Herbartianism has not been written yet, it is possible to say that Ziller's and Rein's educational and political ideas were reactionary regarding liberal reformist claims from 1848 as well as the later formed social-democratic educational programme. This made their pedagogy acceptable and welcome throughout the long restoration period of political and pedagogic development…Ziller's scientistic-Christian belief as a whole can be understood as liberal-conservative while Rein's national-pedagogical tendency pushed Herbartianism more and more towards a conservative and folk block"(1979, 35-36).

We can wholly agree with these findings, but here we have to be careful not to hastily associate Herbartianism with political and ideological conservatism. It seems this connection is very present and rooted in the general perception of Herbartianism. Here we can see an analogy in evaluating Herbartianism with the evaluation of social events in the second half of the nineteenth century. A pattern has been established in pedagogic historiography in which reformist (progressive) pedagogy presents a higher level of the development of pedagogy. The aspirations of reformist pedagogy are labelled in the general pedagogic perception as progressive, and the aspirations of Herbartianism as backward, obsolete and conservative (cf. Klingberg 1998, 121). This perception was undoubtedly aided by reformist pedagogy itself because it needed an opponent for its establishment (Oelkers 1998, 132). Herbartianism was presented as a backward pedagogic doctrine that slowed down pedagogic and social progress. We are used to explaining social

42 This chapter is an expanded and corrected version of an article first published in German (Protner 2008).

conflicts and social movements in the second half of the nineteenth century (and also later) as a clash between conservative and progressive social forces, where simplification leads to equating conservatism and clericalism, progressiveness and liberalism. Because the dominant perception of history holds Herbartianism and conservatism as negative, the result is a granted belief that they are ideally connected and belong together. This may be true to a certain extent, but there is a whole series of historical facts that suggest otherwise: Herbartianism was an integral part of liberal school and political strategy and, according to the analogy above, it should be given a positive qualitative connotation.

## 5.1. Conservative Catholicism and Herbartianism

### 5.1.1. Mahnič's Attitude Towards Lindner

We can find no text in Slovene pedagogic press up to the late 1880s of the nineteenth century which would present and deal with Herbartianism as a complete and dominant pedagogic concept[43]. But this does not mean that it was not present (see Chapter 3). If nothing else, the teacher training college used Lindners textbooks for pedagogy and didactics from their publication onwards; Mich's textbooks were also available in Slovene translation[44]. These textbooks could be labelled as Herbartianist, but their Herbartianist conceptualisation was first pointed out in Slovenia by A. Mahnič (1890), who sharply attacked Lindner in the journal *Rimski katolik*, in 1890. When Herbartianism was mentioned in Slovenia for the first time, it was in the context of critique and rejection. The initiator of this critique was not a pedagogue but a Catholic ideologist.

In the aforementioned publication, Mahnič criticised Lindner's textbooks as anti-religious. His critical basis was the findings that the subject of philosophy is

43 This is true for the publications in the Slovene language. In Ljubljana, they published a German-language journal *Laibacher Schulzeitung* and in 1884 it issued a short article (one and a half pages) with the title On Herbart-Ziller's Didactic Foundations [*Zu den Herbart-Ziller-Stoy'schen didaktischen Grundsätzen*] (1884) which is, to our knowledge, the first mention in Slovenia (but not in the Slovene language) of Herbartianism as a complete and increasingly more established pedagogic system. Although this article points to the familiarity of the author with the current events in the field of pedagogy abroad, this trade press did not feature articles that dealt with distinctively Herbartianism-influenced articles before and also for some years after.

44 Compare Chapter 3. Lessons in all Slovene teacher training colleges were held in the German language.

the most important in the formation of the views of future teachers. This belief was also shared in respect to teacher training and pedagogical instruction. In connection with this, he found that Lindner's textbook was the most widely distributed in Austrian teacher training colleges; the basis of the critique was the finding that Herbartianism lay at the core of this textbook. Furthermore, Mahnič found that "the state obligatory philosophy in Austria…–as it is known by all the world–is Herbart's", and continued, "Herbart is one of the many students of Kant. It goes without saying that he is a rationalist. Rationalism denies any positive religion. Therefore, away with religion in education!" (Ibid., 155). On this basis, Mahnič found that Lindner's textbook was anti-religious: "The writer shows special resolution against the Catholic church; he would totally exclude it from school" (Ibid.). In short, Mahnič attributed Lindner's pedagogy (under the influence and in connection with Free Masons) a liberal political background that pushed religion out of school.

In the next issue of the *Rimski katolik* (similarly as above) Mahnič (1890a) attacked the anti-religious (i.e. liberal orientation) of the association *Union of Slovenian Teacher Societies* in Ljubljana and its newsletter, the pedagogic journal *Popotnik*. Here he was arguing on the basis of references from the mentioned journal that "Slovenian teachers had not come so far in rationalism and paganism as their liberal German or younger Czech generation counterparts but they are on the way where they will soon be at that point" (Ibid., 285).

The state criticised by Mahnič here is also connected with Lindner and Herbart. "But do our 'allies' not know faith anymore?! Yes, they do know it, but only in the sense that their apostles Herbart and Lindner talk about it. Faith, or godliness is 'the highest of all emotions.' This emotion has to be cultivated also in learners but not on the basis of catholic dogmas, but the 'observation of nature'; it is only in this way that their 'faith becomes alive, enlightened, free from dark dreams and empty (womanly) superstition. And let there be no denying of Herbart's views that every religious education is labelled as 'waking religious interest' which is a vague fruit of new German pantheistic, so-called 'Gefühlsreligion' where there is no room for catholic dogma" (Ibid., 289-290). The citation clearly illustrates the radicalism of Mahnič's Catholicism. On the other hand, we can see why Herbartianism could establish itself in the scope of the dominance of liberalism which, although it did not deny religious education, did not place it in the foreground.

Mahnič's critique and accusations in both articles mentioned were answered by T. Romih (1890), the president of the *Union of Slovenian Teacher Societies*. This was not a defence of Herbartianism (and the question is whether it could be identified at all by Romih as a pedagogic concept), but a defence of liberally oriented teachers and, most of all, Lindner. He warned that Mahnič brings discord among Slovene teachers and proved that liberalism does not oppose Christianity, that Slovene teachers want concordant cooperation with the clergy, but that teaching requires knowledge of methodology which priests do not possess. The education of teachers at that time reached a stage (and this can mostly be attributed to Herbartianism, see Chapter 2) where Romih could decisively state the following: "we the teachers are experts in national schools; and we will not cease to demand experts also as supervisors" (Ibid., 259). In his conclusion, he asked the priests who were Lindner's personal friends or pupils if he ever hurt their religious feelings in any way and also defended his pedagogy. Initially, he found it vexing that Mahnič "re-baptised the mental giant Dr. Lindner into a complete atheist[.]" (Ibid. 257).

Mahnič answered Romih's protest with two articles. In the first (Mahnič 1890b), he closely analyses Lindner's understanding of religion and faith. He was proving Lindner's non-Christian and anti-religious course with the use of citations from his *Encyklopedic Manual of Education* [*Encyklopädisches Handbuch der Erziehungskunde*], which is shown by his connection to Kant and Herbart, that he equates and substitutes religion with manners, that he rejects the supernatural essence of Christianity and condemns the upbringing that results from it as too strained, one-sided, and places it alongside pedagogical barbarisms: That he opposes religious dogmas, rejects religious service and gravitates towards protestantism and pantheism. In short, "Lindner misleads young spirits into atheism" and "as long as Herbart and Lindner bring up our teachers, our conscience will not rest" (Ibid., 411).

In the continuation of the polemic, Mahnič (1891) extensively refuted Romih's understanding of liberalism. The essence of liberalism, in his opinion, is in the tendency to be independent from God which, in public affairs, manifests as the separation between the church and state, along with taking control of education. This kind of liberalism, in his opinion, belongs to Lindner, Romih and their allies (Ibid., 182).

Romih (1891) defended himself with the answer in which he refuted Mahnič's argumentation of Lindner's anti-Christian views where he also cited his *Encyclopaedia*. He finished his contribution with a doubt about Mahnič's "scholarliness", his "character" and the following words: "There is no need and purpose to have a longer polemic with this kind of person" (Ibid., 50). The editorial office of the *Popotnik* added to this quotation, commenting that they are of the same opinion "because you cannot succeed with truth and honesty against a wicked twister of truth[.]" (Ibid.).

The last word in this polemic was reserved for Mahnič (1891a). In his article, he analysed Lindner's philosophical, religious and pedagogic views even more thoroughly on the basis of a book printed in Czech and his biography written by Bayer (also in Czech). We have to admit that Mahnič had a very in-depth understanding of Lindner's thought system, his critique and explanation was (from a viewpoint of dogmatic Catholic teaching) consistent and systematic. It is unfortunate that the leading Slovene intellectual wasted his potential and broad knowledge on a fanatic search for heresy and thus definitely extended the divide between the teachers belonging to the liberal and clerical side.

### 5.1.2. Mahnič's Attitude Towards Herbart and his Dispute with Schreiner

Mahnič knew Lindner's system of thought quite thoroughly; he was also well acquainted with Herbart's philosophy. The reason for his debate about Herbart (Mahnič 1893) was the decoration of the hall (where the aforementioned 5th assembly of the *Union of Slovenian Teacher Societies* took place in Maribor in 1893) with pictures of important pedagogues and Slovene writers and the aforementioned Schreiner's lecture with the title *Newest Aspirations for Reformation on the Pedagogic Field.*

The decoration of the hall was very revealing, in Mahnič's words, because it tried to "symbolically express the spirit of the participants" (Ibid., 405). The wall behind the president had an image of the Slovene bishop Anton Martin Slomšek in the middle and the pictures of J. A. Comenius and J. H. Pestalozzi on the sides. Both side walls had pictures of Herbart, the "founder of modern pedagogy" along with pictures of Slovene writers (*Peta skupščina...*, 1893). Mahnič's religious fanaticism can be illustrated with the fact that he found even the pictures of Comenius and Pestalozzi disturbing[45], he was even more outraged about Herbart's picture and Schreiner's words that "'the so-called Herbart's moral ideas do not contradict the spirit of Christianity. Herbart therefore came, with the help of a completely philosophical contemplation and with a completely scientific method, to the same moral ideas which are in the simple way taught by our Saviour" (Mahnič 1893, 405).

45 One year before Mahnič frowned upon the celebration of Comenius on the events at the 300th anniversary of his birth (Mahnič 1892a) because of his philosophical and religious views (more thoroughly discussed by Medveš [1992]). Mahnič (later) warned about Pestalozzi that he is being adopted by Freemasons and says: "Is it proper for a pedagogue–Freemason, the denier of Christ, to also be celebrated in Slovenian language? We do not want Freemason education!" (1896, 94).

Here Mahnič withheld that Schreiner explicitly stressed that he does by no means think "that a teacher should or be allowed to teach morality according to Herbart or that one should neglect religious education. But no intelligent teacher will doubt that morals have to be taught only by simple teachings of the holy Christian faith. Despite this a diligent teacher will not occupy oneself with moral sciences without benefit. This way they will gain a necessary overview of moral ideas which they have to implant into their pupils" (Peta skupščina..., 262). The withholding of Schreiner's input shows Mahnič's tendentiousness and radicalism in the belief that schools should become religious institutions. Hereafter, he argued (on the basis of Herbart's quotations) that his views were non-Christian. Despite the questionable interpretation, we have to admit that Mahnič is one of the best experts of Herbart's philosophy in Slovenia–he was also one of the few who cited him from the primary sources and thus read him in original[46].

Mahnič also found the following words in Schreiner's speech questionable: "Herbart marks the beginning of a new age in the history of education, an age we call scientific. Herbart has the great credit of rising pedagogics to the level of an independent scientific discipline... Herbart found his success in building his own pedagogic system on two strong pillars: on scientific moral studies i.e. ethics, and the study of the soul i.e. psychology...On the road to a higher cause which is shown by religion and ethics the teachers are lead by psychology" (Mahnič 1893, 414). Schreiner continues this quotation by stressing the importance of psychology for the reliable and safe work of teachers, but he summarises: "So that no one ever understands me wrongly, I explicitly add that I do not want to recommend Herbart's psychology; in the opinion of modern psychologists Herbart's psychology stands on false grounds. If God so may, a psychology for which I think will please teacher needs will see the light in a not-so-distant future" (Peta skupščina... 1893, 263). Mahnič mentioned this thought of Schreiner's at the end of his discussion with the comment that if Herbart's psychology is false, then Herbart cannot be given so much credit for the establishment of pedagogy as a science, and therefore, Schreiner's arguments are contradictory.

Mahnič's critique of Herbart's psychology could of course been predicted. Here his critique explicitly uncovered the ideas and ideological context of denouncing Herbart and Herbartianism as a mechanical pedagogic theory. This was a familiar accusation from reformist (progressive) pedagogy but its origin can clearly be found in the incompatibility of Herbartianist psychology with the traditional Christian

46 In contrast, the author observes that primary source citations from Herbart first appear in the 1990s in Slovene scholarly journals.

view on human psyche. "Crucial", in Mahnič's opinion, is Herbart's "basic statement that the human soul has no abilities or natural forces [Fähigkeiten], as thought so far" (Mahnič 1893, 415) and he continues, after presenting the primary characteristics: "According to this psychology the teacher is the absolute master of his pupil to educate him for whatever he chooses...The success of education can be mathematically calculated;...The future character can be thoroughly determined in the teacher's mind with all the characteristics he will stand before his eyes, perfected, within in ten or twelve years. We said: if Herbart's theory is correct, all this necessarily results from it as soon as it is implemented in education. This theory is very tempting for those who cherish little personal freedom and human individuality or none at all. Herbart's theory gives these people a philosophically founded means to suffocate individuality and its manifestations and aspirations in people and mould them into spiritless edges of absolute will. This method is education, executed on the basis of Herbart's philosophy" (Ibid., 416). Other than presenting Herbart's philosophical views here, Mahnič does not refer to Herbart's original works, but to Lindner's encyclopaedic manual.

Mahnič's discussion is the first in Slovenia in which we can find a clear statement that Herbartianism was the dominant discipline in schools: "Herbart's educational mechanism has begun dominating our schools. It seems as if all education from first grade in state schools to higher classes in secondary schools and partly also higher education is placed more and more on the mechanical ideas of Herbart" (Ibid., 417) where a child's soul is a "'tabula rasa' and totally incapable of gaining by itself any kind of knowledge; therefore it is necessary to build everything in it with instruction. Natural capacities are despised and young spirits are bored, their vitality is wiped out." (Ibid., 417-418).

Mahnič also criticised school programmes and the control over teachers on the basis of the critique of mechanical psychology. "This is also the origin of the excessive fragmentation and splitting of school subjects into individual weeks, days, hours and half-hours. The pedantry of school supervisors in this case is in many cases unbelievable. Here it was decided for the poor teacher what to do for whole months ahead, what they have to teach this or that hour, this or that half-hour, from this time to that day. And woe to any teacher if they neglected the order prescribed by the strict master!...According to the supervisor's calculation, every rank of teacher has to produce his result equally among all students as it can be estimated with all certainty how much a machine which has been fed a certain amount of coal or firewood will produce in a certain time...One cannot calculate with the soul of a human being" (Ibid., 418). This is a critique of the school system and formalism which was published a decade after the boom of Herbartianist pedagogic theory in Slovenia.

Herbartianism was apparently recognised in cleric circles as a complete pedagogic discipline even before it gained the response of the wider expert community. In 1892, a participant of the first Slovene catholic meeting thought that the resolutions which were debated were too mild. Among other things, they demanded that Catholic public state schools, Catholic colleges and "Slovenian Catholics should also demand absolutely Catholic secondary schools. What kind of classes are spreading in today's secondary schools! Darwinism, Herbartianism, etc" (I. slovenski… 1892, 283). The efforts to reform teacher education in these circles (from passing liberal school legislation onwards) were directed mainly at strengthening the catechist function of teacher training college, i.e. the formation of private Catholic schools.

## 5.2. The Attitude of Catholic Pedagogues Towards Formal Steps

The ideological and political discrepancies between the teachers on the liberal and Catholic side sharpened in the last decade of the nineteenth century to the degree that common class social activity was made impossible. In 1899, the *Union of Austrian-Yugoslavian Teacher Societies*, which up to that time united all teachers regardless their political affiliation, publicly expressed belonging to the liberal political block. With this action, their newsletter *Učiteljski tovariš* [Teacher Comrade] became the herald of liberally oriented teachers. The cleric camp reacted by founding the journal *Slovenjski učitelj* [Slovene Teacher]. Its first issue was published in December 1899 with the subtitle "Newsletter of Christian-thinking teachers" and Slomšek's image on the cover; at the second Catholic gathering in September 1900, the teacher association called *Slomšek's Association* was established (Bergant 1958, 7; Šuštar 2001, 652). Thus we have two teacher organisations and two journals with distinctly opposite political, ideological and epistemologycal world-views in Slovenia at the turn of the century. – Thus, the journal in which an author chose to publish in helps us identify the author's political affiliation, and thus, the position from which they evaluated Herbartianism.

We have seen how sharply Mahnič criticised Schreiner's speech. But the leading Catholic ideologist could not shake Schreiner's reputation. In the following years, Shreiner established himself in Slovenia as the leading pedagogic authority and under his leadership the idea he propagated in his speech–formal steps–received total affirmation. Schreiner most directly influenced school practise in Lower Styria (Štajerska) and also indirectly in other parts of Slovenia. When Fran

Hubad became the territorial supervisor of (Carniola) Kranjska in 1901 (before this he was the headmaster of the male teacher training college in Ljubljana), formal steps became an essential element of his efforts to improve the quality of the school system in Kranjska (see Chapter 3). His efforts were then supported by mostly liberally inclined teachers, but the bureaucratic pedantry and expert questionability of introducing formal steps ended with a general revolt by those teachers who supported Hubad. From then on, formal steps were inscribed in the Slovene collective pedagogic memory as the synonym for all what was bad about the "old school" (more on this issue in Protner 2001; 2007). But here we are interested mostly in the contribution of Catholic pedagogues to Herbartianist pedagogy.

Although Mahnič defined Catholic perception of Herbartianism as authoritarian, and although it seems that the liberal side had an easier time identifying with it, teachers on the Catholic side could also not avoid elements of Herbartianist pedagogy. The theory of formal steps was, of course, the most attractive. The journal *Slovenski učitelj*, published many articles about formal steps. The prevailing standpoint of Catholic pedagogy on this question can be found in the first volume in which the author wrote in the introduction to the article *"Formal steps" in Catechist Lessons*: "Although Herbart's philosophy is not completely based on Christian philosophy and thus consent cannot be given to all its pedagogic practices, no catechist would overlook his didactic advice.... That which is good can also be received from an advisory if we avoid their errors. Because teachers in the modern age lean more and more on Herbart's philosophical 'formal steps', let also the catechist study them more into detail" (A. K. 1900, 171). He solved the uneasiness because of the discrepancy of Herbart's philosophy and Christianity by stating that "formal steps do not give us content but merely show us the way in which the pupil should learn any kind of subject. Thus they can be very well fitted to catechesis; of course the catechist takes the content from catechism and the Bible as explained by the Catholic church" (Ibid.). In this interpretation, formal steps are completely acceptable as a technical-didactic solution where we can also clearly see the effort to overlook their psychological basis, which was (as we have seen) most questionable to the Catholic side.

In the continuation of the article, the author briefly summarises the content of individual steps (in Rein's interpretation) and clarified the differences between individual Herbartians regarding the number and denomination of formal steps. This was followed by a defence of formal steps against the accusations of some catechists that their use is too wasteful time-wise, that this kind of work is too mechanical and boring for children and that formal steps are oriented too much towards the intellect and too little towards the heart and will. These accusations were refuted by the author, who emphasised similar didactic principles–the difference being that "Herbart's school demands clearly defined paths at always the same steps because it is the most natural in a psychological sense" (Ibid., 187). With respect to the accusation that working with formal steps is too rational, he said the following: "The fact alone that I know and understand something well strongly influences the heart and will" (Ibid.).

It has to be emphasised that the present debate was published before the enforcement of the so called *Munich method* [Münchner Methode] (cf. Offele 1961), which shows that formal steps were a part of professional discussion between catechists (and Catholic pedagogues) even before the initiative given by Heinrich Stieglitz and the circle of Munich reform catechists [Münchner Reformkatecheten], who taught religious education systematically. It was only their activity which raised formal steps in religious education to practically the level official doctrine. In 1902, an article was published in the *Slovenski učitelj* under the title *Reform of Catechesis* (1902), in which the author presented "Munich i.e. Psychological method" as he called it. He pointed out that modern didactics emphasises that it is necessary to take into account the subject of education, i.e. the pupil, and pointed to an article from two years prior (see above), where it was mentioned that "some modern pedagogues started arranging class material in accordance with certain steps, leaning on natural psychological processes in children and that especially Herbart-Ziller's formal steps were applicable" (Ibid., 162). The purpose of his article was to point out innovation and progress on the field of didactic articulation of religious education: "Now we have to report about a new attempt. The catechist society in Munich publicly announced a catechist method last year which they call 'psychological'. This method is the fruit of a diligent two-year study and trials. It was not only approved by one catechist but by the whole society which is 140 strong. This alone recommends the new method" (Ibid.). After, he summarises that this method developed on the basis of Herbart-Ziller's formal steps and it is called psychological because it leans on psychological principles of Christian philosophy. In the end, the author finds that this new method can only be praised in the scientific sense, but there are problems with the practical execution because the method is time consuming and it is hard to find enough suitable stories. He pointed out that formal steps are not useful always and everywhere–this warning can be found in practically all debates about formal steps in Slovenia.

Both above-mentioned articles deal with the use of formal steps in religious education and everything leads to believe that these discussions were written by catechists. But the journal *Slovenski učitelj* was not only meant for catechists–primary and secondary school teachers also published in this journal. A number of articles dealt with the use of formal steps in various subjects and topics. In general, it is possible to find that the didactic form recommended by them does not differ in any way from didactic texts in pedagogic journals with secular views.

Here there is always a certain uneasiness. In 1906, Demšar expressed in his article *On the Transference of Herbart's Formal* Steps that these "formal steps… thoroughly changed classes and that,–this cannot be withheld– also improved it substantially.… But Herbart-Ziller's formal steps have their imperfections which had to show sooner or later if, for no other reason, because they lean on a quite arbitrary conception of the human soul" (Demšar 1906, 244). Otto Willmann, a professor at the University in Prague, was far more in accord with the Catholic pedagogic doctrine and was not thought of as a typical representative of Herbartianism (cf. Breznika 2003). In his article, Demšar stresses that Willman discusses three steps and concluded as such: "It's a pity that we have no lesson plans made with Willmann's formal steps. It would be desirable if one of the renowned pedagogues would tackle this wonderful task" (Ibid., 245) Lesson plans in the circle of Christian pedagogues also retained Ziller's or Rein's structure in the years that followed. But let us return to the presentation of the Munich method.

## 5.2.1. The Enforcement of the Munich Method

In 1906, the journal *Slovenski učitelj* again pointed to the Munich or psychological method with the words: "On catechist meetings this method is winning everywhere, more and more catechists stick to it" (Učna slika… 1906, 201). An example of a lesson plan followed, which was developed by Ferdo Heffler, a teacher of religious education from Zagreb during one of the catechist meetings in Croatia. This lesson plan follows a very typical Herbartianist (Ziller's or Rein's) structure of formal steps. In this time, Heffler became considered a great authority among Slovene catechists. The next year the journal *Slovenski učitelj* published an article in which the author pointed to Heffler's activity in the Croatian catechist movement, his efforts in in modernising catechist education, and his attempts to attract Slovene catechists (G. 1907). The same year a Slovene society was also formed by Slovene catechists. The first gathering they organised also hosted Heffler, who actively joined the debate on teaching methods and unanimously supported the Munich i.e. psychological method.

Slovene catechists were invited to the first Croatian-Slovenian pedagogic-catechist course in Zagreb where Heffler, among other things, also lectured about formal steps (Prvi… 1907). In 1909, Heffler lectured at the third Croatian-Slovenian pedagogic-catechist course in Ljubljana about the third formal step (association) in

Comenyus, Herbart-Ziller "and in service of religious education"; his lecture was met with "tumultuous approval" (III. Slovenskohrvatski… 1909, 231).

The assembly of Croat and Slovene catechists in Zagreb in 1911 speaks to how deeply Herbartianist theory of formal steps had rooted itself in religious education. M. Dovranič argued in his speech to make textbooks and syllabuses in accordance with the concentratio, and pointed out the meaning of association (Čadež 1911, 217). The influence of Herbartianist pedagogy could also bee seen in the fourth Croatian-Slovenian catechist course held in Pazin in 1914. Here Heffler's paper on the history and development of the psychological method was read. The reporter summed up Heffler's paper as follows: "Professor Heffler proves that the leading method of teaching from St. Augustine onward was the one which is now unjustly called the 'Munich' method and lists individual advocates i.e. representatives of this way of teaching. Today there is probably no catechist who would not approve of the importance of the 'Munich teachings'. The Vienna catechist Viljem Pichler even sanctioned this method with his new book which was loudly greeted and approved by the catechist board" (Čadež 1914, 188).

## 5.3. The Attitude of Liberals Towards the Reception of Formal Steps on the Catholic Side

The recognition of the Munich method (1901) coincides with the appointment of Fran Hubad as state school upervisor in Carniola (Kranjska). He aspired to reform education based on formal steps. His aspiration collapsed only a few years later (1903/1904) with the theoretical polemic[47] between Hubad and Viktor Bežek (later the headmaster of the teacher training college in Gorica[Goriza]) about formal steps, in which Bežek rightfully pointed to the bureaucratisation and professional questionability of introducing formal steps into school practise (cf. also Protner 2007). The majority of (liberally inclined) teachers were on Bežek's side at this point, and although *formal steps* had already been present in teacher education for a long time, after that point, the liberal educational press did not discuss them anymore. The debate about formal steps was still present in Catholic educational press (as we have seen above). This did not go unnoticed by the liberal side.

In 1909, an anonymous author in the journal *Učiteljski tovariš* ended his commentary with ridicule (of the already mentioned) third Croatian-Slovenian catechist

47 It is one of the more well-known polemics in the history of Slovenian pedagogy. See Chapter 3.

course in Ljubljana, mostly relating to Heffler's ideas. He wrote: "We did not want to believe our eyes, is it the truth or are we dreaming" (Najnovejši... 1909, 1) and then cited from Heffler's lecture titled *Third Formal Step (Association) in Komensky-Herbart-Ziller. He finished srcastically in the Service of Religious Education*: "We say openly that we are glad for these lines of text. Here we were able to read honest words spoken by a man-professional who does not always speak of 'religion' and 'religion' and which were written by a honest reporter catechist A. Čadež as editor. Literal paragraphs are at last *the most brilliant celebration of ideas of big thinkers– pedagogues Comenius, Herbart and Ziller*!" (Ibid., 2, emphasis in original).

Thereafter the writer first reminded the readers of Schreiner's 1893 lecture at the assembly of *Union of Slovenian School Societies* about newest aspirations for reformation on the pedagogic field,[48] and after this, of Mahnič's reaction: "And this lecture infuriated Dr. Mahnič who at that time still edited the late '*Rimski katolik*' so much that he published a passionate discussion in the same journal under the title *Herbart The Philosopher about Modern School*. The discussion can be found in the 4th publication from 1893 and is written in Mahnič's genre. We were reminded of this discussion by the report on the third catechist meeting in the 10th edition of the journal 'Slov. učitelj'.–We would be happiest to simply show it as an example–of how everything comes around and changes. Yes, yes, the teachers of Slovenia were at that point 16 years ago, the catechists of Slovenia only adopted this position in 1909, they had to be brought to this view by a Croatian expert" (Ibid., 2-3). This scornful remark that Slovene catechists were a decade and a half behind (liberal) teachers in implementing what they then criticised is followed by a longer quotation of Mahnič's introduction, which ended with the author cynically observing that "the conviction issued at that time by the fanatic Mahnič about Slovenian teachers because of Herbart is also valid in full measure for the Slovenian catechists on the third meeting. And thus our paths merged. We are in good company!" (Ibid., 3).

The article proves the findings that Herbartianism (especially the teachings about formal steps) was introduced into catechism later than in other places but it was at least on a theoretical level, also more frequently defended, which shows how modernisation was introduced also where lessons remained more traditional.

48 This lecture was commented on as follows: "The main idea of this lecture was grounded on Herbart's teachings and pedagogy. This lecture was very instructional and thorough and quite modern for that time because this was the time when Herbartianism started gaining broad approval due to Ziller" (Najnovejši... 1909, 2).

On the other hand, the author's statement that Slovene catechists were "the ones who mainly form the 'Slomšek group' [and] became enthusiastic Herbartians" (Ibid.) was exaggerated. The article is provocative and must be understood in the context of the cultural struggle between the liberal and cleric teachers. As it suggests on the one side, *Slomšek's association* turned to Herbartianism, it can also be understood on the other hand, that the liberal teachers still held on to Herbartianism, as the author does not reject formal steps. Both are misleading. On both sides, and especially in their journals, Herbartianism was outset by new pedagogic developments and schools of thought. Let us, in conclusion, look at the reaction of catholic pedagogues to these events.

## 5.4. The Encounter of Herbartianism and New Pedagogic Developments Through the Eyes of Catholic Pedagogues

A kind of synthesised view on the introduction of new pedagogic developments can be found in 1914 in the journal *Slovenski učitelj* in the article *Pedagogic Streams* (Fabinc 1914). Fabinc found that the methods of Herbart's school were based on Herbart's psychology, "which has today been proven as false", that formal steps "which are only a natural consequence of this intellectual theory are really something thought-out and it is their contribution that didactics rose incomparably high in comparison with the former century", but that it is "the fault of Herbart-Ziller's school that our public education floats in a totally intellectual current" (Ibid., 24). This current in his opinion achieved its peak at the time of the polemic between Hubad and Bežek. "From this time on, the enthusiasm for this field, which they wanted to declare officially as infallible, is diminishing. A couple of years ago it could not even be thought that the whole pedagogic stream would flow along Herbart's ideas in such a short time" (Ibid.).

The author (rightly) found that this turn was initiated by experimental (progressive) pedagogy "which opened a new perspective[,] particularly in psychological development and the life of our child" (Ibid.). The inductive method, which entered psychology and didactics through the natural sciences, had a lot of success in his opinion. Here he adds: "But we must not forget that the direction and essence of classes will always be determined by the religious and philosophical views of society" (Ibid., 25). This warning urges a certain distance towards experimental pedagogy. In this scope, he wrote that A.W. Lay gathered with his experimental pedagogy "a whole lot of material,...but the learned dismiss his theory...as non-scientific[.]" (Ibid.). In his critiques, he mentions P. Barth and O. Meßmer, who pointed out that "today's school with its clarity is deficient because it despises reaction in every impression... With this we are at working school, propagated mainly by Kerchensteiner's stream. It should also be mentioned that this stream also has a lot of humbug and empty theoreticism which will never be realised" (Ibid.).

Apart from the findings of experimental pedagogy, which are very helpful for classes in his opinion, the author stresses the fact that modern pedagogy is merging into voluntarism, which can also be seen in education. "How different are the apperception theories of Herbart and Wundt alone. In Herbart apperception is only association and assimilation, in Wundt it is an act of will, the result of carefulness" (Ibid.). But uneasiness is also present here because he points out that Wundt is "an important person in modern psychology but not a friend of Christian ethics" (Ibid.).

The Catholic pedagogues who followed modern scientific streams and tried to implement them in Catholic educational doctrine faced a difficult task: How to reconcile the old doctrine with new scientific findings, and at the same time ensure the preservation of tradition? The author found a solution in Foerster's pedagogy. "Foerster is a likeable spectre among modern pedagogues who came closest to Christianity. Self-overcoming is the principle of all his education and its utmost virtue. Today, this means a lot or even everything. In his opinion, school must bring back freedom to a person so as to allow the spirit to rule over the body, the central human over the peripheral one. He pledges for the reform of school discipline which is inadequate. Our schooling system should adopt ideas which came from America, mostly school-city with its 'Self-Government' of pupils" (Ibid., 26).

# 6. Herbartianism Between Normality and Excess in the Case of the Lesson Plan Titled "The Cat"[49]

The Slovene school museum in Ljubljana has been featuring museum lesson plans in its program for many years–the lessons of our grandparents[50]. Visitors to the museum have the opportunity to choose a lesson (they offer five different thematic fields from 1880 to 1930) and can participate as virtual students in a reconstructed, authentic classroom environment. Among the lessons, we can find a lesson called "The Cat" [Mačka], which features an elementary-level, natural science class from around 1907. I have unfortunately not seen one of these lessons in person, but I could make out from discussion with the museum management that these classes were selected more by chance than on the basis of expert judgement. The class contains simple content representative of every elementary class, and the original didactic instructions for this class were also available. Although the choice was made rather arbitrarily by the organisers, they ended up choosing a class that was heavily debated during the first decade of the nineteenth century–even part from the debate of Herbartianist didactic theory in everyday school practise at schools in Ljubljana. The origins of the critique of this class dates back to 1903, when there was a heated dispute about formal steps in the Slovene pedagogic press (see Chapter 3). The class about the cat was mentioned for the first time in context with this polemic. We cannot find any reasoning why it was the cat because children then learned about other animals with the use of the same didactic logic. The class about the cat, however, was also later mentioned by critics, and this raises our attention. It turns out that it is possible to illustrate the transition of Herbartianism from normality to excess with an analysis of references to this class.

---

49 This chapter is an expanded and corrected version of an article first published in German (Protner 2010a).

50 "Slovenski šolski muzej," http://www.ssolski-muzej.si/slo/pedagogueactivity.php?item=51.

## 6.1. From Creative Innovativeness to Rigid Repressiveness: From Normality to Excess

### 6.1.1. The Last Decade of the Nineteenth Century: The Story of the Success of Herbartianism

In Slovenia, Herbartianism as a conscious pedagogic concept emerged rather late compared to its presence in, for instance, Germany, Switzerland and Austria (see Chapter 3). But this had some advantages. Henrik Schreiner, in his debate from 1893 (see Chapter 4), already had reflected on the polemic, which was set off on the topic of Herbartianism abroad; in the same lecture he also refuted with ridicule some of the extremist Herbartianist ideas. In terms of Herbartianism in Slovenia, it is characteristic that it followed the ideas of the opposition inside Herbartianism more because the first articles and all of which followed already featured a critique of the rigid and mechanical use of formal steps and some of the most controversial ideas (cultural-historical epochs, concentration) of Ziller's school. This direction contributed to the fact that teachers (initially more or less in Lower Styria /Štajerska/) accepted formal steps and introduced them as a useful methodological innovation, helped improve the quality of classes.

The organisational framework of these events can be summed up as follows (cf. Chapters 3 and 4):

When Schreiner took over the headmaster's position at the Maribor Teacher Training College in 1890, became the centre of innovative theoretical and applied pedagogy in Slovenia. The first Slovene discussion was written by a teacher at the practice teaching school of Maribor Teacher Training College (Majcen 1891). This is not only the first domestic expert discussion about formal steps. The level of expert discussion and scientific apparatus employed also represent a turning point in the the Slovene scholarly press. As headmaster and district school supervisor, Schreiner was the first to gain the support of the teachers at the College for the new concept. He was also able to attract support from public school teachers of his district. As an important speaker at Slovene teacher conferences, he was further able to raise the concept to the level of school reform.

It was as early as 1892 when Schreiner suggested a new concept of readers at the territorial teacher conference. It was a concept (cf. Chapter 4) that Schreiner did not mention the following year (1893), when he discussed the implementation of formal steps and concentration of lessons at the conference of the *Union of Slovenian School Societies*, but the following year (1894) at this same conference, he introduced a concept of the new textbook conceptually in line with the theory of formal steps and concentration of lessons. A year later in 1895, the *Memorandum of the Union of Slovenian School Societies* was passed regarding the reorganisation of public school readers, which brought the idea to the level of programme demand in relation to educational reform in Slovenia. In 1899, Schreiner initiated the founding of the Slovene publishing company for expert pedagogic literature, over which he also presided. The publishing company editorial policy promoted textbooks that contained formal steps. Thus, his work at the publishing company also enabled the practical execution of the new concept. The only thing missing was a new reader in line with the new concept–Schreiner and Fran Hubad provided for this in 1902 (cf. Protner 1999a, 2010).

The essential quality of this period cannot be solely attributed to the fact that Herbartianist theory was being introduced. More importantly, Schreiner succeeded in exciting and motivating first his colleagues, the teachers of the district he supervised, and finally, all Slovene teachers for the new concept. This process unfolded as a form of democratic professional and scholarly discussion, which included the teachers from the beginning. Schreiner did not demand that the teachers of his district to introduce formal steps. Instead, he motivated them to the degree that they became interested in studying this new didactic method, debated it, and started promoting it within the pedagogic press. While this was happening in Lower Styria (Štajerska), the situation in Carniola (Kranjska) was fundamentally different. The stereotype about the negative attitude towards Herbartianism cannot be simply generalised to all of Slovenia.

### 6.1.2. The First Decade of the Twentieth Century: Herbartianism as a Constraint

When Fran Hubad became the county school supervisor for Carniola (Kranjska) in 1902 after leaving his position as headmaster at the teacher training college in the capital of Carniola (Kranjska)–Ljubljana–he started his work with the honest intention to improve education in a territorial known as one of the worst developed in the Monarchy (see Chapter 3). Schreiner and he knew each other well and it is obvious that he wanted to implement the model of formal steps in Carniola (Kranjska), which Schreiner had applied in Lower Styria (Štajerska). But this was a completely different story here and this experience is an important message to all who work to reform education by introducing new didactic approaches. Hubad also wanted to present the debate on introducing formal steps to the district teacher conferences, i.e. into the legally prescribed form of expert gatherings of teachers intended to train educators in new didactic methods and introduce improvements into school practise, but he introduced this discussion with a decree. In the following couple of years, formal steps were the topic of all teacher conferences in the territory. All the teachers had to make lesson plans for the conferences; the school supervisors then inspected and evaluated them and appointed a teacher to give a mock lesson in front of the colleagues. These additional requirements not only demanded extra time and effort on the part of the teachers, but also placed an additional burden during an economic recession, which had lowered teacher salaries. Growing dissatisfaction was recorded by Viktor Bežek, who wrote in his article from 1903 that teachers in Ljubljana were telling him about a school supervisor who enters in the middle of a class and asks the teacher at which formal step they are currently at in the lesson, which triggered a heated debate with Hubad. From then on, Herbartianism in the Slovene pedagogic consciousness is stigmatised as a pedagogic concept that demands rigid, mechanical instruction.

## 6.2. The Class About the Cat as an Illustration of the Degeneration of Herbartianist Theory

I started my research into Herbartianism some years back by firstly forming a general opinion of the topic in the German-speaking region. My first basic discovery was that Herbartianism is something completely different than Herbart's pedagogic theory; it also became evident how contentious the generally established negative stereotype about Herbartianism was. Because I did not have domestic studies, I researched the presence and development of Herbartianism in Slovenia by chronologically reviewing the domestic pedagogic press and literature from 1869 on. The process of trying to answer the question why Herbartianist pedagogic doctrine has been written into the historical memory in such a negative way first required scouring volumes upon volumes in order to identify the texts that in any way related to Herbartianism.

The origins of this negative image started to present themselves as I browsed the pedagogic journals from the year 1903 (cf. Protner 1999). I have already mentioned that this is the year when the domestic theoretical polemic about formal steps broke out. But it turns out that the negative image does not come from theoretical refusal, but from the practise of introducing formal steps. This was namely the same year when Engelbreht Gangl, the editor of the newsletter of liberally inclined teachers (i.e. the majority of teachers) published an article in which he pointed out that it was "Hubad's era" when teachers were loaded with more and more work and the district supervisors had endless control over the work of teachers.

In the end, he also indicated an expert-theoretical critique. He wrote: “Formal steps and the so-called formulated sentences, the treasures of our lesson plans, go nicely hand in hand. Formulated sentences are without doubt the high-end of modern methodology. If it is written: ‘A cat has a head, a body and limbs’, but the pupil says: ‘A cat has limbs, a body and a head’, someone can come and say with whole earnestness and strictness: ‘Your teaching methods are worthless–and therefore everything is worthless!’” (Gangl 1903, 217).

This is the first time we come across “the cat” and we can easily read the context from the citation. I am not interested in the analysis of the didactic execution–the author’s scornful tone is much more revealing because it illustrates his attitude towards the deficient school practise. But the citation nevertheless does not reveal what we can imagine from the expression “formal sentences”, although it seems that the author mentions them in a way as if it would be clear and obvious to all readers–as it actually was at that time to teachers of Ljubljana. Later, I will present a lesson plan that illustrates the function of formal sentences, but first, let us look at other mentions of the cat. It is quite interesting that the cat is mentioned two years later in an article titled *Bureaucracy at School* by an author from the other side of the debate, in the cleric camp: “You like to hear when the children clatter various formal sentences during the supervisions. The most typical are, of course, from the illustrative teachings, let us say, from the one about the cat. ‘A cat is a domestic animal. A cat has a head, body, limbs and a tail’ as they have to learn from the illustrative teachings, the same goes for all other subjects. Thus the folk school supervisory is more a military discipline or official revision where the outlook is more important–whether the buttons shine enough, whether a hat is not placed too far towards the forehead; are the formal books kept, the numbers match, etc.” (Štrukelj 1907, 200).

Both citations point to an atmosphere and a problem that arose during the implementation of formal steps in Carniola (Kranjska). But several volumes had to be browsed before a complete picture of events in the school and pedagogy of that time emerged, which followed the reformist efforts of a new district school supervisor. The feelings of teachers was described by the article where the anonymous author strongly attacked the district school supervisor of Ljubljana (his name was Anton Maier) and described the events and his actions after Hubad took over the territorial supervision. Because we have already discussed this (see Chapter 3), we will now focus on the cat, which was also present. The basic critique the author addresses to Maier was that he judged the quality of the class on the basis of how the teacher used formal steps: “Who showed Maier formal steps during his class–was a good teacher; he got an absolution of all his sins! Pardon me–he had to have one more thing: willow branches soaked in water and sprouting grain on every school window...The schools of Ljubljana were at that time discussing that poor cat, so that its fur flew in all directions, but the reformist capabilities also flew past the sprouting grain and soaked willow branches" (Maierjevci 1911, 1).

The author of the following article was even more explicit when he reveals the events around 1902:

"It was a long time ago when somebody–and this was not Maier–made, let us say, a good lesson plan titled 'Mačka' [The Cat]. There was joy in Jerusalem that someone from the Maier circle was able to make something good! The lesson plan 'Mačka' was presented to the interns; they rounded them all up in the Ljubljana College of education–male and female–they had an teacher observation and with it the fortune to have seen and heard the lesson plan 'Mačka'. I mentioned this famous cat already but it has to be observed once more today because it is a classic! Maier at once took hold of it and appointed the cat as the first and main point of first class.–We have nothing against this lesson plan and also nothing against this domestic animal being discussed in first class. But this should not be repeated year after year and in all first classes of Ljubljana at once! If Maier were a pedagogue he would have prepared such a detailed plan which would enable every teacher to make their own work–to their own taste, their individuality and according to real needs! This year this, next year something else...First year this lesson plan was well placed and good! The following years it was less appropriate because of the following reason. According to Maier's super-pedagogy the formal sentences from this lesson plan must be learned by every pupil. Thus, when the time is ripe for the cat, these formal sentences of the cat echo in all first grades of Ljubljana schools; they reverberate on all hallways, penetrate into the street, in chorus in the morning and in the afternoon; on Monday, Tuesday, Wednesday, Friday and Saturday–always and as long as every pupil really learns all the formal sentences about the cat with the help of this beautiful method of Maier's. But the cat really does not have such power to qualify every pupil for the next grade! Despite the cat, every first grade has 6, 8, or 10 pupils who have to repeat the year. Next year 'the time' comes again when the cat is on! As soon as the teacher brings a stuffed cat into the classroom, 6, 8, or 10 stand up and shout: 'I know, I know!' The teacher of course cannot alter the teaching system...

'So you also know the cat?' - the teacher asks.

'Yes, my sista taught me [sic]!'

'And me my blother [sic]!'

Oh, agony! Now generate the interest for a topic which half of the class already know...

I could write whole books about the numbskull things this person brought together in his lesson plans-even such which he adopted for press, let alone the others!" (Maierjevci 1911a, 1-2).

Again, the scornful tone is more revealing than the actual facts. But we can form a relatively detailed impression of the school practise, which officially referred to itself to Herbartianist theory, on the basis of the citation. At the end of the citation, we can even find a hint about the "numbskull" ideas in the lesson plans Maier published in written form. The self-evident next step is thus to find the book mentioned and look at the lesson plan about the cat. We can find it in the manual for teachers with the title *Lesson Plans from the Illustrative Teachings for the 1st and 2nd grade* in which Maier was the editor and wrote the preface (Maier 1906). Here Maier explains that the book brings "the minimal detailed lesson plan for the teachings in the first and second grade. It differs substantially from the multitude of books of the same sort where there is far too much content. The teacher has to first select and adapt the appropriate content for their needs from these kinds of books. This is of course far from easy and demands a lot of effort and skill. This is why the teachers really missed books which definitely define the teaching material which would also be applicable in first two school years" (Ibid., n.p.). How much the teachers really missed this kind of book is of course debatable. As is the case today, teachers' autonomy in planning and running classes was also widely accepted at that time (this can also be found in the citation above). This kind of autonomy was also publicly sought after by teachers. But on the other hand, we can imagine that some teachers found this kind of directness a kind of relief in their work because these types of books offered easy pedagogic recipes.

According to Maier, the book was intended mostly for schools in Ljubljana; with smaller changes they could also be used in other schools. He explained that the first issue (Maier 1903) was published on the basis of an agreement o the teachers of Ljubljana in 1903, when they decided that the teachers will prepare a detailed syllabus for didactics in the following year. They had numerous consultations with the supervisor for this purpose: "Under the direction of the supervisor it is essential to form mainly a minimal lesson plan; then sentences were formed which should be developed during class. On the basis of this individuals made lesson plans under the newest methodological standards and these were then thoroughly examined and partially also practically tested" (Ibid.).

Despite the apparent democracy, there is a striking thought that the minimal detailed curriculum was formed on the basis of instructions from the supervisor, that it was Maier who determined the content of this plan. The term "formal sentence" is also very interesting. In the quotation above they were mentioned by an anonymous author who wrote: “In accordance with Maier’s super-pedagogy the formal sentences of this lesson plan have to be learned by all pupils” Maierjevci 1911a, 1). We can deduce from Maier’s preface that formal sentences are logically connected to the newest methodological principles (he is of course talking about formal steps). This is a concept that cannot be found by the leading Herbartians and it is possible that this was Maier’s idea. We can deduce from the example shown later on that this is a variety of the fourth formal step designated as “recapitulation” [Zusammenfassung] according to Rein. Among other things, this formal step was designed to “reinforce the conceptual with the transfer of it in the form of theorems, examples of rules, sample sentences into a systematic whole which is a support for the content” (Rein, 1903, 147). Here we can also add Rein’s explanation that “the forms of spoken expression for gaining conceptual results cannot be forced upon pupils” (Ibid., 148) and that it is necessary to “shield the pupils against routine spoken and memory knowledge” (Ibid., 149).

A completely different emphasis in comparison to the Herbartianist doctrine (Rein) can be found in Maier’s preface. “Repetitio est mater studiorum” was the motto of his book (Maier 1906) and this was also pointed out in the initial part of the book. “The most important for content for every subject of the explicit lessons is that it is arranged correctly and then spoken in appropriate sentences in standard language which the pupils can understand. The sentences formed accordingly have to be repeated until every pupil knows them…The material has to be diligently repeated” (Ibid., 7).

Here we can get the picture of a school that we might identify as “old school”. A wholesome insight into this kind of school is portrayed by the lesson plans found in Maier’s book. Let us examine the lesson plan from the illustrative teachings in the first school year titled *The Cat* more in detail.

First we find the listed teaching props: a stuffed cat with a mouse in its mouth, pictures of cats playing, a cat which hunts a mouse in the kitchen, a specimen of a cat’s head and the food mice eat (flour, sugar, etc.).

Next there is a list of *formal sentences* in the bold print:

**“A. The description of the animal from a biological point of view.**

**1. A cat is a domestic animal.**

**2. It hunts for mice which it grabs in a leap.**

**3. Its paws have sharp claws”**… [and so forth through no. 13] (Ibid., 31, emphasis in original)

This is followed by a description of the animal’s biological state which is divided into preparation, announcement of the aim, teaching new material and summary of the lecture. This is followed by the second part of the material (the description of characteristic parts of the body) which has the same form as teaching new material and finishes with the summary of the second part of the presented teaching material and the revision of the whole material. In the end there is also a short story and two drawings of a cat in different positions and two sketches of the basis for drawings (a circle and an ellipse).

To get an idea of what Maier's critics had in mind, let us look at this lesson plan in greater to detail. The beginning of the lesson is as follows:

"**Preparation.** How do we call animals which we keep at home? (Domestic animals.) – List some according to size. (Domestic animals are: horse …)

**Announcement of the aim.** Kids! Today we want to talk about the cat.

**Teaching new material.** The cat was listed among the animals we keep at home. So, what kind of animal is the cat, N?

**A cat is a domestic animal.**

*Repeat, A! - B! - C!*

*I want to repeat once again myself, and then all of you will repeat!*

Be**gin!**" (Ibid., 32, emphasis in original).

The bold print in the word "begin" means that the teacher has to strongly stress the second syllable. The notion of such classes is additionally illustrated by Maier's instructions (in the initial theoretical part) about what the pronunciation in joint revisions and individual pupil revisions should be. "When pupils speak in a chorus, they should not make pauses between individual syllables, but between words, i.e. The - cat - is - a - domestic - animal. In the second year we talk jointly in such a rhythm which individuals would need in speech. For this purpose let only one pupil speak with the correct pronunciation at first, i.e. The **cat** is a do**mes**tic **a**nimal" (Ibid., 2, emphasis in original).

Not only does the lesson plan dictates the content of the class in a form of sentences to be spoken by teachers and pupils–the lesson plan also thoroughly suggests the spoken pronunciation and rhythm.

Later, the discussed lesson plan lists questions for the teachers to pose (and the answers that should be given by the pupils), which lead toward the next "formal sentence":

"Why do we have a horse, N? (The horse pulls the cart.)

Why the cow, O? (The cow gives milk.)

Why the dog, P? (The dog watches the house and goes hunting with the hunter.)

And why do we have the cat (pointing to the cat with a mouse in its mouth)? (The cat hunts mice.)

What is on this picture, S? (Kittens.)

What is this one doing? (Licking milk.)

And this one? - What about this one?

Kids especially like young cats. Sometimes they also tease them. They tie a piece of paper on a string and drag it around the room. Who has ever done something like this? - What does the cat do first when it sees something moving on the floor? (It crouches on the floor.) - And then what? (Then it jumps towards the paper.) - Why does it do that? (Because it likes to play.) - Why else does it do that? (Because it thinks the piece of paper on the string is a mouse.)

Where do mice live? (In holes.) Who has seen a mouse hole? - Where? (In a wall.) - And you, F? (In the ground.)

I would like to tell you how the cat hunts for mice. Listen!

The cat sits behind the mouse hole, so that the mouse does not see it immediately, and waits. When the mouse's head appears out of the hole, the cat crouches. As soon as the poor mouse leaves the hole and starts running around the room, the cat jumps on top of it (showing the picture) and grabs it. The mouse squeals and squeals and twists but cannot escape.

What does the cat do when the mouse starts running around the room, R? (It jumps towards it.)

So remember:

**It hunts for mice which it grabs in a leap.**

Repeat, A! - B! - C!

I want to repeat once again myself, then all of you will repeat!

Be**gin!**" (Ibid., pp. 32-33, emphasis in original).

This pattern is repeated from the first to the last "formal sentence" within the description of animals from a biological point of view. Before the transition to the schematic description, we find the summary of a lecture, which looks like this:

"Now we want to revise!

1. Because we keep a cat in the house, whit kind of animal is it?
2. What does it do?
3. What does it have on its paws?
4. What kind of teeth does it have?
5. What do you know about the cat's vision?
6. What kind of hearing does the cat have?
7. What helps it during hunting for mice?
8. Because the cat hunts for mice, which are a pest, whit kind of animal is it?

(Repeat five or six times.)

Who can say it on their own without me asking questions?

(The pupil repeats, the teacher points to the picture or object and in this way supports the pupil during answers.)" (Ibid., 35).

The lesson plan presented belongs to the frame of "descriptive illustrative teaching" by finishing with a story and drawing of a cat, which apparently represents the phase of application. The banality of this story and the moral-educational effect to be achieved with such lessons require special analysis.

## 6.3. Conclusion

Herbartianist pedagogic doctrine was also accompanied by a very strong critique at the height of its popularity, and with the development of reformist (progressive) pedagogy, this critique only increased. A negative critical attitude towards Herbartianism was typical for a long time in the pedagogic historiography and it is only the last couple of decades that this attitude has gradually begun to change. The analysis of the most well-known representatives of Herbartianism (i.e. Ziller and Rein) shows that their theoretical views cannot be equated with the pedagogic practise in the period of dominance of Herbartianist doctrine, the presentation of authors who were thought of as the alternative within Herbartianism deviated from this image even more. One of these was, for example, K.V. Stoy. The inconsistency of his pedagogic ideas and the school practise he implemented is nicely illustrated with the cliché representation of the weaknesses of Herbartianism by Rotraud Coriand, that even Lev Nikolajevič Tolstoj "praised Stoy's private school especially because of the spirit present there" (2000, 206).

The school from the end of the nineteenth and the beginning of the twentieth century operating in the spirit of Herbartianism could have had this or that image. We could say that Herbartianism covers all stages between pedagogic normality and deviance. How Herbartianism manifested itself in school practise was not as much dependent on the theory that it referred to (the Herbartianist theory is extraordinarily heterogeneous), but mainly on the social, and most of all, state-administrative context in which it took hold. Thus we have on the one hand, the image of Herbartianism in which teachers accepted it as a reasonable, professionally justified and useful reform. When it was being introduced teachers cooperated as partners. On the other hand, we have the image of Herbartianism as a bureaucratic constraint established not to improve teachers' skills, but to subordinate educators to administration dimensions of school work.

Every complete pedagogic concept has the potential to hover between normality and deviance. By entering from theory into practise, it is never possible to unambiguously claim what the theory is actually about. This steers us toward a paradoxical thought that only what deviates from pedagogic norm can be normal, because only this enables the participation of those who have to practise it. And vice versa: Consistent observance of a norm (in connection with constraint) definitely leads toward deviance of the one and the same norm.

# Bibliography


"I. slovenski katoliški shod v Ljubljani." *Popotnik* 13 (1892): 248–250, 263–266, 281–284.

"III. slovenskohrvatski pedagoški in katehetski tečaj v Ljubljani (Poročilo o referatih)." *Slovenski učitelj* 10 (1909): 229–223, 249–252, 271–274.

A.K. "„Formalne stopinje" pri katehetičnem pouku." *Slovenski učitelj* 1 (1900): 171–174, 187–189, 204–207, 217–221, 233–236.

Adam, E. "Die Bedeutung des Herbartianismus für die Lehrerbildung in der österreichischen Reichshälfte der Österreichisch-Ungarischen Monarchie mit besonderer Berücksichtigung des Wirkens von Gustav Adolph Lindner." In: *Delo in pdagogoški nazori Henrika Schreinerja*, ed. E. Protner, 227-241. Maribor, Slovenia: Univerza v Mariboru 2002.

Adam, E. "Die Pädagogik des Herbartianismus in der Österreichisch-Ungarischen Monarchie. Eine Forschungskizze." In *Die Pädagogik des Herbartianismus in der Österreichisch-Ungarischen Monarchie*, ed. E. Adam and G. Grimm, 5–20. Vienna, Berlin: Lit Verlag, 2009.

Adl-Amini B., J. Oelkers, and D. Neumann. "Grundlinien des pädagogischen Herbartianismus." In: *Pädagogische Theorie und erzieherische Praxis*, ed. B. Adl-Amini B., J. Oelkers, and D. Neumann, 11–48. Bern, Stuttgart: Verlag Paul Haupt, 1979.

"American Herbartians." Accessed 3 March 2014. http://www.yushodo.co.jp/ydsc/list2012_7/2404042.pdf (3.3.2014)

Arbeitsstelle für Internationale Herbartianismusforschung. Accessed 10 November 2013. http://www.uni-due.de/herbartianismus-forschungsstelle/Start.shtml.

Arbeitsstelle für Internationale Herbartianismusforschung. "Abgeschlossene Projekte." Accessed 18 November 2013. https://www.uni-due.de/herbartianismus-forschungsstelle/Projekte.shtml.

Asmus, W. "Der unbekannte Herbart." *Pädagogische Rundschau* 2 (1948): 68–75.

Asmus, W. "Herbarts Pädagogik des Charakters." *Internationale Zeitschrift für Erziehungswissenschaft* 6 (1950/51): 256–261, 398–404.

Asmus, W. *Johan Friederich Herbart, Eine pädagogische Biographie, Der Lehrer, 1809-1841*. Part II. Heidelberg: Quelle & Meyer, 1970.

Asmus, W. "Anmerkungen." In *Pädagogisch-didaktische Schriften*, ed. W. Asmus, vol. 3 of *Johann Friedrich Herbart: Pädagogische Schriften*, 347–411. 2nd unaltered ed. Stuttgart: Klett-Cotta, 1982

Bellerate, B. M. *J. F. Herbart und die Begründung der wissenschaftlichen Pädagogik in Deutschland*. Hannover et al.: Herman Schroedel Verlag, 1980.

Benner, D. "Einleitung." In *Johann Fredrich Herbart: Systematische Pädagogik*, ed. D. Benner, 13–52. Stuttgart, Germany: Klett-Cotta, 1986.

Benner, D. "Einzelinterpretation der Texte." In *Johann Fredrich Herbart: Systematische Pädagogik*, ed. D. Benner, 239–390. Stuttgart: Klett-Cotta, 1986a

Bergant, M. *Poizkusi reforma šolstva pri Slovencih*. Ljubljana: DZS, 1958.

Bezjak, J. "Bežek v pravdi za 'formalne stopnje'". *Popotnik* 41 (1920):_ 222–242.

Bezjak, J. *Občna zgodovina vzgoje in pouka s posebnim ozirom na ljudsko šolstvo za moška in ženska učiteljišča*. Ljubljana: Kr. zaloga šolskih knjig in učil, 1921.

Bežek, V. "O formalnih in didaktiških stopnjah in pa o razvijajoče-upodabljajočem pouku." *Popotnik* 24 (1903): 1–5, 33–42, 65–73, 134–154, 202–210, 235–246.

Bežek, V. "Ad interim!." *Popotnik* 24 (1903a): 97–104.

Bežek, V. "Ad interim!." Pt. 3. *Popotnik* 24 (1903b): 161–185.

Bežek, V. "Moj odgovor." *Popotnik* 25 (1904): 1–15, 46–57, 65–75.

Blankertz, H. *Die Geschichte der Pädagogik. Von der Aufklärung bis zur Gegenwart*. Wetzlar, Germany: Büchse der Pandora, 1982.

Bliedner, A. *Karl Volkmar Stoy und das pädagogische Universitätsseminar*. Leipzig: Georg Reichardt Verlag, 1886.

Brezinka, W. *Pädagogik in Österreich: Die Geschichte des Faches an den Universitäten vom 18. bis zum Ende des 20. Jahrhunderts*. Vol. 1, *Einleitung: Schulwesen, Universitäten und Pädagogik im Habsburger Reich und in der Republik; Pädagogik an der Universität* Wien. Vienna: Verlag der Österreichischen Akademie der Wissenschaften, 2000.

Brezinka, W. *Pädagogik in Österreich: Die Geschichte des Faches an den Universitäten vom 18. bis zum Ende des 20. Jahrhunderts*. Vol. 2, *Pädagogik an der Universitäten Prag, Graz und Innsbruck*. Vienna: Verlag der Österreichischen Akademie der Wissenschaften, 2003.

Brezinka, W. Pädagogik in Österreich: Die Geschichte des Faches an den Universitäten vom 18. bis zum 21. Jahrhundert. Vol. 3, *Pädagogik an der Universitäten Czernowitz, Salzburg und Linz*. Vienna: Verlag der Österreichischen Akademie der Wissenschaften, 2008.

Brezsnyiánszky, L. "Der kontinentale Einfluß auf die ungarischen Erziehungswissenschaft und Lehrerbildung um die Jehrhundertwende." In *Delo in pdagogoški nazori Henrika Schreinerja*, ed. E. Protner. Maribor, Slovenia: Univerza v Mariboru, 2002.

Brzoska, H. *Die Notwendigkeit pädagogischer Seminare auf der Universität und ihre zweckmäßige Einrichtung*. Leipzig: Verlag von Johan Ambrosius Barth, 1836.

C. “Iz mariborske okolice.” (Hospitacija). *Popotnik* 18 (1897): 285–287.

Ciperle, J. “Pedagogični pogovori.” *Učiteljski tovariš* 17 (1877): 113–117.

Coriand, R., and M. Winkler, eds.: *Der Herbartianismus: die vergessene Wissenschaftsgeschichte*. Weinheim, Germany: Deutscher Studien Verlag, 1998.

Coriand, R. “Karl Volkmar Stoy – ein Herbartianer?” In *Der Herbartianismus, die vergessene Wissenschaftsgeschichte,* ed. R. Coriand and M. Winkler, 15–29,. Weinheim, Germany: Deutscher Studien Verlag, 1998a.

Coriand, R. *Karl Volkmar Stoy und die Idee der Pädagogischen Bildung*. Würzburg, Germany: Ergon, 2000.

Coriand, R., ed. *Herbartianische Konzepte der Lehrerbildung*. Bad Heilbrunn, Germany: Verlag Julius Klinkhardt, 2003.

Coriand, R. *Pädagogischer Herbartianismus. Fachsystematische Bibliographie für datenbasierte Grundlagenforschung*. Vol. 1, *Philosophische Pädagogik*. Jena, Germany: Verlag IKS Garamond, 2010.

Coriand, R.: *Pädagogischer Herbartianismus. Fachsystematische Bibliographie für datenbasierte Grundlagenforschung*. Vol. 2, *Historische Pädagogik, Praktische Pädagogik, Metaebene: Fachsystematische Fragen und Gesamtdarstellungen*. Jena, Germany: Verlag IKS Garamond, 2010a.

Coriand, R., G. Böhme, and K. Henkel. “Bio-doxographisches Korpus Pädagogischer Herbartianismus–Zwischenergebnisse eines DFG-Projekts als Kooperationsimpuls.” In *Herbartianische Konzepte der Lehrerbildung: Geschichte oder Herausforderung*?, ed. R. Coriand, 269–297. Bad Heilbrunn, Germany: Klinkhardt, 2003.

Coriand, R., K. Grundig de Vazquez, K. Henkel, and G. Böhme G. “Alphabetische Bibliographie pädagogischer Herbartianismus,” last modified 24 January 2014. https://www.unidue.de/herbartianismusforschungsstelle/Bibliographie.shtml.

Coriand, R., K. Henkel. “Zeitschriftenbibliographie,” last modified 24 January 2014. https://www.uni-due.de/herbartianismus-forschungsstelle/Zeitschriftenbiblio.shtml.

Coriand, R., K. Henkel, and G. Böhme. “Lebenskizzen ausgwählter Herbartianer,” last modified 24 January 2014. https://www.uni-due.de/herbartianismus-forschungsstelle/Skizze.shtml.

Cruikshank, K. “Der Einfluß der Herbartianer auf die Lehrerausbildung in den USA, 1880-1920.” In *Der Herbartianismus- die vergessene Wissenschaftsgeschichte*, ed. R. Coriand and M. Winkler, 99–108. Weinheim, Germany: Deutscher Studien Verlag, 1998.

Čadež, A. "Skupščina katehetov v Zagrebu." *Slovenski učitelj* 12 (1911): 193–196, 217–219.

Čadež, A. "Katehetski tečaj v Istri." *Slovenski učitelj* 15 (1914): 187–190.

Černej, L. "Samodelavnost pri pouku." *Popotnik* 15 (1894): 260–264

Darroch, A. *Herbart and the Herbartian theory of education: A criticism*. London et al.: Longmans, Green, and Co., 1903.

Demšar, J. "O preosnovi Herbartovih formalnih stopenj." *Slovenski učitelj* 7 (1906): 243–245.

"Didaktični formalizem." *Popotnik* 25 (1904): 33–46.

Dietering, P. *Die Herbartische Pädagogik vom Standpunkte moderner Erziehungsbestrebungen gewürdigt*. Leipzig: Fritz Eckardt Verlag, 1908.

Dodd, C.I. *Introduction to the Herbartian Principles of Teaching*. Whitefish, Montana: Kessinger Legacy Reprints, 2010. First published 1898 by Swan Sonnenschein & CO Limited, and The MacMillan Company.

Dollinger, B., F. Eßer, C. Müller, M. Schadbach, and W. Schöer. *Sozialpädagogik und Herbartianismus. Studien zu einem theoriegeschichtlichen Zusammenhang*. Bad Heilbrunn, Germany: Klinkhardt, 2010.

Driesch, J., J. Esterhues. *Geschichte der Erziehung und Bildung*. Vol. 2. Paderborn, Germany: Schöning, 1964.

Dumbović, I. "Stjepan Basariček (1848-1918) utemeljitelj hrvatske pedagogije–doprinos osposobljavanju učitelja." In *Delo in pedagogoški nazori Henrika Schreinerja*, ed. E. Protner, 271–287. Maribor, Slovenia: Univerza v Mariboru, 2002.

Dunkel, H. B. *Herbart and Herbartianism: An Educational Ghost Story*. Chicago and London: The University of Chicago Press, 1970.

Engelbrecht, H. *Geschichte des österreichischen Bildungswesens. Von 1848 bis zum Ende der Monarchie*. Pt. 4. Vienna: Österreichischer Bundesverlag, 1986.

Fabinc, F. "Pedagoške smeri." *Slovenski učitelj* 15 (1914): 24–27.

Felkin, H. M. and E. *An Introduction to Herbart's Science and Practice of Education*. Boston: D. C. Heath & co., 1900.

Franković, D. "Počeci Herbartovog pedagoškog utjecaja u Hrvatskoj." *Savremena škola* 15 (1961): 172–193.

Fröhlich, G. *Die wissenschaftliche Pädagogik Herbart-Ziller-Stoy in ihren Grundlehren gemeinfaßlich dargestelt und an Beispielen erläutert*. 7th ed. Vienna & Leipzig: Verlag von A. Pichlers Witwe & Sohn, 1901. 1st ed. published 1883.

G. "Reforma katehetičnega pouka." *Slovenski učitelj* 3 (1902): 161–164, 181–182, 209–211.

G. "Katehetsko gibanje na Hrvaškem." *Slovenski učitelj* 8 (1907): 10–12.

Gangl, E. "V obrambo." *Učiteljski tovariš* 43 (1903): 209–211, 217–218, 241–243.

Gabršek, F. "Vzgojni pomen pouka." *Učiteljski tovariš* 27 (1887): 17.

Geissler, E. E. *Herbarts Lehre vom erziehenden Unterricht*. Heidelberg: Quelle & Meyer, 1970.

Gestrin, F., and V. Melik. "Demokratčna in socialna prebuja na Slovenskem." In *Zgodovina Slovencev*, ed. Z. Čepič and D. Nećak, 527–597. Ljubljana: Cankarjeva založba, 1979.

Gleißner, A. "Die Münchner Methode im Spegel zeitgenössischer Auseinandersetzungen." In *Katehetische Blätter* 112 (1987): 429–432.

Gönner, R. *Die österreichische Lehrerbildung von der Normalschule bis zur Pädagogischen Akademie*. Vienna: Österreichischer Bundesverlag für Unterricht, Wissenschaft und Kunst, 1967.

Gönner, R. "Der Herbartianismus in Österreich." In *Jahrbuch der österreichischen Pädagogischen Gesellschaft als Festschrift zum 70. Geburtstag von o.ö. Universitätsprofessor Hofrat Dr. Ulrich Schöndorfer*, ed. A. Eder, M. Heitger, and K. Wolf, 41–53. Vienna: Österreichischer Bundesverlag für Unterricht, Wissenschaft und Kunst, 1969.

Grimm, G. "Gustav Adolf Lindner als Wegbereiter der Pädagogik des Herbartianismus in der Habsburgermonarchie." In *Die Pädagogik des Herbartianismus in der Österreichisch-Ungarischen Monarchie*, ed. E. Adam and G. Grimm, 21–35. Vienna, Berlin: Lit Verlag, 2009.

Groothoff, H. H. *Funktion und Rolle des Erziehers*. Munich: Juventa Verlag, 1972.

H. "Maribor." *Popotnik* 12 (1891): 310–312, 323–324, 341–342.

H. "Metodiška obravnava pesmi 'Ilirska tragedija'". *Slovenski učitelj* 2 (1901): 85–89, 101–103.

H.P. "Dr. Karol Kehr." *Učiteljski tovariš* 25 (1885): 106–108.

Hayward, F. H., and M. E. Thomas. *The critics of Herbartianism and other matter contributory to the study of the Herbartian question*. London: Swan Sonnenschein & co., 1903

Hayward, F. H. *The secret of Herbart: an essay on education and a reply to Professor James of Harvard*. Swan Sonnenschein & co., 1904

Herbart, J. F.: "Die ersten Vorlesungen über Pädagogik" (1802). In *Johann Friedrich Herbart: Pädagogische Schriften*, ed. W. Asmus, pt. 1, *Kleinere pädagogische Schriften*, 2nd unaltered ed., 121–131. Stuttgart: Klett-Cotta, 1982.

Herbart, J. F. *The Science of Education; Its General Principles Deducated from its Aim and the Aestetic Revelation of the World* (1806). Translated from the German with a biographical introduction by Henry M. and Emmie Felkin. Boston: D.C. Heath & co., 1896.

Herbart, J. F. "Allgemeine Pädagogik aus dem Zweck der Erziehung abgeleitet" (1806). In *Johann Friedrich Herbart: Pädagogische Schriften*, ed. W. Asmus, pt. 2, *Pädagogische Grundschriften*, 2nd unaltered ed., 9–155. Stuttgart: Klett-Cotta, 1982.

Herbart, J. F. "Annahme der Berufung nach Königsberg" (1808). In *Johann Friedrich Herbart: Pädagogische Schriften*, ed. W. Asmus, pt. 3, *Pädagogisch-didaktische Schriften*, 2nd unaltered ed., 9–12. Stuttgart: Klett-Cotta, 1982.

Herbart. J. F. "Entwurf zur Anlage eines pädagogischen Seminars" (1809). In *Johann Friedrich Herbart: Pädagogische Schriften*, ed. W. Asmus, pt. 3, *Pädagogisch-didaktische Schriften*, 2nd unaltered ed., 13–18. Stuttgart: Klett-Cotta, 1982.

Herbart, J. F. "Bericht über die Einrichtung eines didaktischen Instituts" (1810). In *Johann Friedrich Herbart: Pädagogische Schriften*, ed. W. Asmus, pt. 3, *Pädagogisch-didaktische Schriften*, 2nd unaltered ed., 18–20. Stuttgart: Klett-Cotta, 1982.

Herbart, J. F. "Plan der Errichtung eines Hauslehrerinstituts für die Provinz Ostpreußen" (1810a). In *Johann Friedrich Herbart: Pädagogische Schriften*, ed. W. Asmus, pt. 3, *Pädagogisch-didaktische Schriften*, 41–43. Stuttgart: Klett-Cotta, 1982.

Herbart, J. F. "Über erziehung unter Öffentlicher Mitwirkung" (1810b). In *Johann Friedrich Herbart: Pädagogische Schriften*, ed. W. Asmus, pt. 1, *Kleinere Pädagogische Schriften*, 2nd unaltered ed., 143–151. Stuttgart: Klett-Cotta, 1982.

Herbart, J. F. "Vorschlag zur Erweiterung des didaktischen zu einem pädagogischen Institut (1815)." In *Johann Friedrich Herbart: Pädagogische Schriften*, ed. W. Asmus, pt. 3, *Pädagogisch-didaktische Schriften*, 2nd unaltered ed., 20–23. Stuttgart: Klett-Cotta, 1982.

Herbart, J. F. "Entwurf zu einem Reglement für das pädagogische Seminar" (1821). In *Johann Friedrich Herbart: Pädagogische Schriften*, ed. W. Asmus, pt. 3, *Pädagogisch-didaktische Schriften*, 2nd unaltered ed., 24–28. Stuttgart: Klett-Cotta, 1982.

Herbart, J F. "Die Nothwendigkeit [sic] pädagogischer Seminare auf der Universität und ihre zweckmässige Einrichtung. Von Dr. Heinr. Gust. Brzoska, Prof. an der Universität zu Jena, Leipzig 1836 (1836)." In *Johann Friedrich Herbart's Pädagogische Schriften*, ed. O. Willmann, pt. 2., 2nd ed., 270–273. Leipzig: Verlag von Leopold Voss, 1880.

"Herbartianism," *Encyclopaedia Britannica*, accessed 5 September 2013. http://www.britannica.com/EBchecked/topic/262691/Herbartianism.

"Herbartizem," *Slovenski večjezični terminološki slovar vzgoje in izobraževanja*, accessed 6 September 2013. http://www.termania.net/slovarji/terminoloski-slovar-vzgoje-in-izobrazevanja/3474481/herbartizem?query=herbartizem.

Hubad, F. "Ad interim!" II. *Popotnik* 24 (1903): 129–133.

Hubad, F. "Kranjski pristaši formalnih stopenj in njih kritik." *Popotnik* 24 (1903a): 193–202, 225–234, 257–269, 289–301, 321–333, 358–361.

Hüllmann. K. D. "Plan der Errichtung eines Hauslehrerinstituts für die Provinz Ostpreußen" (1810). In *Johann Friedrich Herbart: Pädagogische Schriften*, ed. W. Asmus, pt. 3, *Pädagogisch-didaktische Schriften*, 2nd unaltered ed., 41–43. Stuttgart: Klett-Cotta, 1982.

"Iz krškega okraja" (conference). *Popotnik* 13 (1892): 253.

"Iz mariborske okolice." *Popotnik* 17 (1896): 220.

J. K. "Ovca." *Slovenski učitelj* 14 (1913): 204–207, 225–227.

Jacobs, F. *Die religionspädagogische Wende im Herbartianismus*. Heidelberg: Quelle & Meyer, 1969.

Javornik, M., and M. Šebart. "Herbartov koncept vzgoje." *Sodobna pedagogika* 42 (1991): 138–147.

Johnston, W. M. Österreichische Kultur- und Geistesgeschichte. Gesellschaft und Ideen in Donauraum 1848-1938. Vienna: Böhlau, 1974.

Klingberg, L. Herbartianismus: Paradigma, Schule, Exempel." In *Der Herbartianismus: die vergessene Wissenschaftsgeschichte*, ed. R. Coriand, 115–125. Weinheim: Deutscher Studien Verlag, 1998.

Koprivnik, J., and G. Majcen. *Začetnica za slovenske ljudske šole*. Vienna: C. kr. založba šolskih knjig, 1897.

Koschnitzke, R. *Herbart und Herbartschule*. Aalen, Germany: Scientia Verlag, 1988.

Kržič, A. "Stališče katehetske metode." *Slovenski učitelj* 8 (1907) 156–161, 184–187.

Kržič, A. "Psihologija in pedagogika." *Slovenski učitelj* 9 (1908): 56–59, 77–79, 106–108, 172–180.

L. "Še nekaj učnih slik." *Slovenski učitelj* 4 (1903): 5–9.

Lapajne, I. "Zgodovina pedagogije." *Učiteljski tovariš* 27 (1887): 19–20, 34–36, 50–53, 66–68, 82–84, 98–100, 115–118, 132–134, 146–148, 162–165, 179–181, 195–198, 211–214, 227–229, 244–247, 258–261, 275–277, 291–293.

Lesjak, D. "Ciril in Metod. Učna slika po formalnih stopnjah za višjo skupino." *Popotnik*, 18 (1897): 198–201, 216–217.

Levičnik, A. "Katehetski shod." *Slovenski učitelj* 8 (1907): 136–141.

Lichtenwallner, M. "Formalne stopnje." *Popotnik* 18 (1897): 132–134, 148–151, 164–170.

Lindner, G. A. *Allgemeine Erziehungslehre*. Vienna: Verlag von A. Pichler's Witve & Sohn, 1877.

Lindner, G. A. *Allgemeine Unterrichtslehre*. Vienna: Verlag von A. Pichler's Witve & Sohn, 1877a.

Magerle I. "Nekateri novejši pojavi na našem šolskem polju." *Popotnik* 25 (1904): 161–171.

[Mahnič, A.]. "Slovenski katoliški shod. Ljudska šola pa ljudski učitelji." *Rimski katolik* 2 (1890): 152–161.

Mahnič, A. "Slovenski katoliški shod." *Rimski katolik* 2 (1890a): 282–294.

Mahnič, A. "Dr. G. A. Lindner. Slovenskim učiteljskim 'zaveznikom'." *Rimski katolik* 2 (1890b): 403–413.

Mahnič, A. "Kaj je prav za prav liberalizem?" *Rimski katolik* 3 (1891): 17–22, 182–189.

Mahnič, A. "'Kristjan' dr. Lindner." *Rimski katolik* 3 (1891a): 380–395.

Mahnič, A. "Internacijonalna slovesnost Jana Amosa Komenskega." *Rimski katolik* 4 (1892): 65–82.

Mahnič, A. "Bodi luč! – slaviteljem Komenskega." *Rimski katolik* 4 (1892a): 136–147.

Mahnič, A. "Filozof Herbart v novodobni državni šoli." *Rimski katolik* 5 (1893): 405–421.

[Mahnič, A.]. "Čigav je bil Pestalozzi?" *Rimski katolik* 8 (1896): 94–95.

Maierjevci. *Učiteljski tovariš* 51, no. 31 (1911): 1–2.

Maierjevci. II. *Učiteljski tovariš* 51, no. 32 (1911a): 1–2.

Maier, A., ed. *Učne slike iz nazornega nauka za I. in II. razred*. Ljubljana: L. Schwentner, 1903.

Maier, A., ed. *Učne slike iz nazornega nauka za I. in II. razred*. 2nd altered ed., Ljubljana: L. Schwentner, 1906.

Maier, H. *Die Geschichte des Vereins für wissenschaftliche Pädagogik*. Leipzig: Felix Meiner Verlag, 1940.

Majcen, G. "Psihologično-metodična utrditev učne slike 'Iznajdba knjigotiskarstva'." *Popotnik* 12 (1891): 51–54, 69–71, 85–87, 99–100, 118–120, 167–170, 207–209, 287–288.

Majcen, G. "Iznajdba knjigotiskarstva." *Popotnik* 12 (1891a): 9–12, 23–26, 41–43.

"Maribor." *Popotnik* 12 (1891): 341.

"Maribor." (Zborovanje). *Popotnik* 17 (1896): 346–347.

"Maribor." *Popotnik* 18 (1897): 110.

M. C. "Iz mariborske okolice." *Popotnik* 17 (1896): 220.

M. C. "Iz mariborske okolice." *Popotnik* 17 (1896a): 258–259.

McMurry, C. A. *The Elements of General Method: Based on the Principles of Herbart*. New York and London: MacMillan & Co, 1903.

Medveš, Z. "Antropozofski temelji waldorfske pedagogike." *Sodobna pedagogika* 40 (1989): 228–242.

Medveš, Z. "Interpretacije nazorov Jana Amosa Komenskega pri Slovencih." *Sodobna pedagogika* 43 (1992): 118–134.

"Mejnik." *Slovenski učitelj* 10 (1909): 49–52.

Metz, P. *Herbartianismus als Paradigma für Professionalisierung und Schulreform*. Bern et al.: Peter Lang, 1992.

Mi-ci. "Zadnja naša hospitacija." *Popotnik* 19 (1898): 94.

Mich, J. *Občno vzgojeslovje*. Trans. F. Gabršek. Ljubljana: "Pedagogiško društvo" in Krško, 1887.

Mich, J. *Občno ukoslovje*. Trans. F. Gabršek. Ljubljana: "Pedagogiško društvo" in Krško, 1888.

Müller, E. *Das Paradigma des Herbartianismus unter problemgeschichtlichem Aspekt*. Dr. phil dissertation: Pädagogischen Hochschule Erfurt. Erfurt, 2000.

"Najnovejši Herbartovci." *Učiteljski tovariš* 48, no. 47 (1909): 1–3.

Neumann, D., J. Oelkers. "'Verwissenschaftlichung' als Mythos? Ligitimationsprobleme der Lehrerbildung in historischer Sicht." *Zeitschrift für Pädagogik* 20 (1984): 229–252.

Nohl, H. "Der lebendige Herbart. Vortrag bei der reformpädagogischen Tagung des Göttinger Instituts für Erziehung und Unterricht am 18. März 1984." *Die Sammlung 3* (1984): 201–208.

Oelkers, J. *Die Vermittlung zwischen Theorie und Praxis in der deutschen Pädagogik von Kant bis Nohl. Eine ideengeschichtliche Untersuchung*. Dr. phil dissertation: University of Hamburg. Hamburg, 1975.

Oelkers, J. "Das Ende des Herbartianismus. Überlegungen zu einem Fallbeispiel der pädagogischen Wissenschaftsgeschichte." In *Rekonstruktionen pädagogischer Wissenschaftsgeschichte*, ed. P. Zedler and E. König, 77–116. Weinheim, Germany: Deutscher Studien Verlag, 1989.

Oelkers, J. "Wilhelm Rein und die Konstruktion von »Reformpädagogik«." In *Der Herbartianismus: die vergessene Wissenschaftsgeschichte*, ed. R. Coriand and M. Winkler, 129–154. Weinheim, Germany: Deutscher Studien Verlag, 1998.

Offele, H. W. *Geschichte und Grundlagen der sogenannten Münchener katechetischen Methode; Die methodische Erneuerung im ketechetischen Unterricht*. Munich: Deutscher Katechetenverein, 1961.

Osterwalder, F. *Pestalozzi: ein pädagogischer Kult. Pestalozzis Wirkungsgeschichte in der Herausbildung der modernen Pädagogik*. Weinheim und Basel: Beltz, 1996.

Peček, M. "Strokovna avtoriteta osnovnošolskega učitelja v drugi polovici 19. stoletja." Šolska kronika. Zbornik za zgodovino šolstva in vzgoje 5 (1996): 69–78.

"Peta skupščina 'Zaveze slovenskih učitelljskih društev' v Mariboru." *Popotnik* 14 (1893): 209–210, 241–244, 257–263, 278, 290–294, 305–312, 324–327.

"Peta štajerska učiteljska konferenca." *Popotnik* 13 (1892): 275–278, 289–291, 306–308.

Pohl, H. E. *Die Pädagogik Wilhelm Reins*. Bad Heilbrunn, Germany: Verlag Julius Klinkhardt, 1972.

"Pokorščina." *Učiteljski tovariš* 18 (1878): 26–27, 40–42.

Prange, K. "Zillers Schule. Wissenschaftliche Pädagogik am Beispiel des 'Leipziger Seminarbuchs'." In *Rekonstruktionen pädagogischer Wissenschaftsgeschichte*, ed. P. Zedler and E. König, 21–41. Weinheim, Germany: Deutscher Studien Verlag, 1989.

"Predavanje v 'Slovenski Šolski Matici'." *Učiteljski tovariš* 43, no. 12 (1903): 95.

Protner, E. "Herbartov univerzitetni pedagoški seminar." Šolska kronika 5 (1996): 55–68.

Protner, E. "Herbartizem na Slovenskem do 1. svetovne vojne." Šolska kronika 7 (1998): 87–110.

Protner, E. "Nadzornik Anton Maier in formalne stopnje." Šolska kronika 8 (1999): 16–31.

Protner, E. "Vpliv herbartizma na reformo osnovnošolskih beril v obdobju pred 1. svetovno vojno." *Sodobna pedagogika* 50 (1999a): 16–31.

Protner, E. *Herbartistična pedagogika na slovenskem (1869-1914)*. Maribor, Slovenia: Slavistično društvo, 2001.

Protner, E., ed. *Delo in pedagoški nazori Henrika Schreinerja*. Maribor, Slovenia: Univerza v Mariboru, 2002.

Protner, E. "Schreinerjev prispevek k razvoju pedagogike in šolstva na Slovenskem." In *Delo in pedagoški nazori Henrika Schreinerja*, ed. E. Protner, 71–83. Maribor, Slovenia: Univerza v Mariboru, 2002a.

Protner, E. "Pädagogischer Takt und Lehrerpersönlichkeit in herbartianischen Konzepten der Lehrerbildung." In *Herbartianische Konzepte der Lehrerbildung: Geschichte oder Herausforderung*?, ed. R. Coriand, 205–223. Bad Heilbrunn: Klinkhardt Verlag, 2003.

Protner, E. "Das Verhältnis der katholischen Pädagogen zur Herbartianischen Pädagogik auf slowenischem Gebiet." In *Pädagogische und kulturelle Strömungen in der k. u. k. Monarchie*, ed. J. Hopfner and A. Nèmeth, 103–131. Frankfurt am Main et al.: Peter Lang, 2008.

Protner, E. “Herbart’s university pedagogical seminar.” In *Education from the past to the present: Pedagogical and didactic lessons from the history of education*, ed. J. Hopfner and E. Protner, 105–121. Bielsko-Biała et al.: Filozofska fakulteta, Mednarodna založba Oddelka za slovanske jezike in književnosti, 2009a.

Protner, E. “Die Formalstufen und die „Verdammung“ des Herbartianismus am Beispiel Sloweniens.” In *Die Pädagogik des Herbartianismus in der Österreichisch-Ungarischen Monarchie*, ed. E. Adam and G. Grimm, 113–130. Vienna: Lit Verlag, 2009.

Protner, E. “Volksschullesebuch als Mittel der Etablierung der herbartianistischen Pädagogik in Slowenien.” *Neveléstörténet* 7 (2010): 134–143.

Protner, E. “Herbartianismus zwischen Normalität und Exzess am Beispiel des Unterrichtsbildes der »Katze«.” In *Normalität, Abnormalität und Devianz. Gesellschaftliche Konstruktionsprozesse und ihre Umwälzungen in der Moderne*, ed. A. Nóbik and B. Pukánszky, 59–71. Frankfurt am Main et al.: Peter Lang, 2010a.

Protner, E. “La formazione degli insegnanti in Slovenia e l‘applicazione „ragionevole“ dell‘herbartismo.” In *La scuola degli Asburgo: pedagogia e formazione degli insegnanti tra il Danubio e il Po (1773-1918)*, ed. S. Polenghi, 241–263. Turin, Italy: Società editrice internazionale, 2012.

“Prvi hrvatskoslovenski pedagoškokatehetski tečaj u Zagrebu.” *Slovenski učitelj* 8 (1907): 89–93, 105–106.

R. “Na grobeh.” *Slovenski učitelj* 3 (1902): 319–323.

R. “Trapec.” *Slovenski učitelj* 4 (1903): 136–137, 150–152.

Radeka, I. “Odnos kulturne prema herbartističkoj pedagogiji u Hrvatskoj.” In *Delo in pdagogoški nazori Henrika Schreinerja*, ed. E. Protner, 251–267. Maribor, Slovenia: Univerza v Mariboru, 2002.

Randels, G. B. *The Doctrines of Herbart in the United States*. Ph.D. thesis: University of Pennsylvania. Philadelphia, 1909. https://archive.org/details/doctrinesofherba00rand.

Rein, W. “Pädagogisches Universitäts-Seminar.” In *Encyklopädisches Handbuch der Pädagogik*, ed. W. Rein, pt 6, 2nd ed., 531–546. Langensalza, Germany: Hermann Beyer & Söhne, 1907.

Rein, W., A. Pickel, and E. Scheller. *Theorie und Praxis des Volksschulunterrichts nach Herbartischen Grundsätzen. Das erste Schuljahr*. 7th ed. Leipzig: Verlag von Heinrich Bredt, 1903. 1st ed. published 1878.

Richter, K. *Die Herbart-Zillerschen formalen Stufen des Unterrichtes nach ihrem Wesen, ihrer geschichtlichen Grundlage und inhrer Anwendung im*

*Volksschulunterrichte*. 3rd supplemented ed. Leipzig: Max Heffes Verlag, 1908. 1st ed. published 1887.
"Rjavi hrošč." *Slovenski učitelj* 6 (1905): 102–107, 123–126.
Romano, D. F. "Der Beitrag Herbarts zur Entwicklung der modernen Psychologie. Eine geschichtskritische Analyse." In *Johann Friederich Herbart: Leben und Werk in den Widersprüchen seiner Zeit*, ed. W. Busch and H. D. Raapke, 89–103. Oldenburg, Germany: Heinz Holzber Verlag, 1976.
Romih T. "'Rimskemu katoliku' v odgovor." *Popotnik* 11 (1890): 257–160.
Romih, T. "'Rimskemu katoliku' namesto odgovora." *Popotnik* 12 (1891): 49–50.
S. J. "Učna slika." *Slovenski učitelj* 5 (1904): 105–107.
Scheffler, H. *Zillers Formalstufentheorie und der Vorwurf des unterrichtmetodischen Schematismus*. Kastellaun, Germany: Aloys Henn Verlag, 1977.
Schmidt, V. *Pedagogika, III, Skripta Višje pedagoške šole v Ljubljani*. Ljubljana: Višja pedagoška šola, 1949.
Schmoranzer, J. "Henrik Schreiner." *Pedagoški letopis*, 10–28. Ljubljana: Slovenska šolska matica, 1920.
Schreiner, H. "O koncentraciji pouka v ljudski šoli." *Popotnik* 13 (1892): 2–4, 19–23.
Schreiner, H. "Schulnachrichten." In *Erster Bericht der k. k. Lehrerbildungsanstalt in Marburg*, ed. H. Schreiner, 63–79. Marburg, Slovenia: Verlag der k. k. Lehrerbildungsanstalt, 1892.
Schreiner, H. "Schulnachrichten." In *Zweiter Bericht der k. k. Lehrerbildungsanstalt in Marburg*, ed. H. Schreiner, 1–28. Marburg, Slovenia: Verlag der k. k. Lehrerbildungsanstalt, 1895.
Schreiner, H., and F. Hubad. Čitanka za obče ljudske šole. Pt. 2. (Za drugo in tretje šolsko leto štiri-in večrazrednih ljudskih šol.) Vienna: V cesarski kraljevi zalogi šolskih knjig, 1902.
Schreiner, H. *Analiza duševnega obzorja otroškega in duševlovni proces učenja. Nauk o formalnih stopnjah*. Ljubljana: Slovenska šolska matica, 1903.
*Schulordnung für die Seminarschule zu Jena*. Jena, Germany: Verlag des pädagogischen Seminars, 1858.
Schwenk, B. *Das Herbartverständnis der Herbartianer*. Weinheim, Germany: Julius Beltz, 1963.
Schwenk, B. "Probleme der Herbart-Nachfolge." In *Herbart Interpretation und Kritik*, ed. B. Gerner, 113–130. Munich: Ehrenwirth, 1971.
"Schul- und Unterrichtsordnung für die allgemeinen Volksschulen." In *Verordnungsblatt für den Dienstbereich des Ministeriums für Cultus und Unterricht*, 501–516. Vienna: Verlag des k. k. Ministeriums für Cultus und Unterricht, 1870.

"Seznam knjig, izdanih in založenih po Slovenski šolski matici [priloga]." *Pedagoški zbornik*. Ljubljana: Slovenska šolska matica, 1940.

Šilih, G. "Ob stoletnici rojstva Henrika Schreinerja." *Nova obzorja* 3 (1950): 665–668.

Šilih, G. "Pedagoško delo Henrika Schreinerja." *Sodobna pedagogika* 2 (1951): 218–231.

Soldt, J. *Karl Volkmar Stoy und die Johann Friedrichs-Schule zu Jena. Ein Beitrag zur geschichte der Pädagogik und Lehrerbildung in Deutschland*. Weimar: Verlag Hermann Böhlaus Nachf., 1935.

"Spomenica „Zaveze slovenskih učiteljskih društev", tičoča se preosnove ljudskošolskih čitank." *Popotnik* 16 (1895): 161–165.

Stoy, K. V. *Organisation des Lehrerseminars. Ein beitrag zur methodologie der Pädagogik angeknüpft an eine historische einleitung und berichterstattung über das erste lebensjahr des Lehrerseminars zu Beilitz*. Leipzig: Verlag von Wilhelm Engelmann, 1869.

Stoy, K. V. *Encyklopädie, Methodologie und Literatur der Pädagogik*. Leipzig: Verlag von Wilhelm Engelmann, 1878.

Strmčnik, F. "Razvoj izobraževanja osnovnošolskega učiteljstva na Slovenskem v obdobju od leta 1869 do razpada Avstro-Ogrske." In *Osnovna šola na Slovenskem 1869–1969*, ed. V. Schmidt et al., 339–441. Ljubljana: Slovenski šolski muzej, 1970.

Štrukelj, I. "Birokratizem v šoli." *Slovenski učitelj* 8 (1907): 198–200.

Šuštar, B. "Verska šola in liberalni duh učiteljev." In *Melikov zbornik: Slovenci v zgodovini in njihovi srednjeevropski sosedje*, ed. V. Rajšp et al., 635–654. Ljubljana: Založba ZRC, ZRC SAZU, 2001.

Tancer, M. *Slovenski pedagoški klasik Henrik Schreiner*. Maribor, Slovenia: Univerza v Mariboru, Pedagoška fakulteta, Raziskovalni inštitut, 1990.

Tancer, M. "Življenje in delo Henrika Schreinerja." In *Delo in pedagoški nazori Henrika Schreinerja*, ed. E. Protner, 11–20. Maribor, Slovenia: Univerza v Mariboru, 2002.

Teml, H. "Die Lehrerbildung nach dem Reichsvolksschulgesetz." In Österreichische Bildungs- und Schulgeschichte von der Aufklärung bis zum Liberalismus. Jahrbuch für österreichische Kulturgeschichte. Vol. 4. Eisenstadt, Austria: Institut für österreichische Kulturgeschichte, 1974.

"Učna slika po psihološki metodi." In *Slovenski učitelj* 7 (1908): 201–203.

Ufer, C. *Introduction to the Pedagogy of Herbart*. Authorized translation by J. C. Zinser from the 5th German ed., under the auspices of the Herbart club, ed. Charles De Gamo. Boston: D. C. Heath, 1894.

“Ukazi in odredbe šolskih oblastev.” *Učiteljski tovariš* 42 (1902): 170–171, 185.
V. B. “Metodiška obravnava Aškerčeve pesmi „Čaša nesmrtnosti“”. *Slovenski učitelj* 2 (1901): 67–76.
V. B. “Nekaj učnih slik.” *Slovenski učitelj* 3 (1902): 288–290, 305–307, 335–337, 352–354, 368–371.
Volpicelli, I. *Herbart e i suoi epigoni. Genesi e sviluppo di una filosofia dell'educazione*. Turin, Italy: UTET Università, 2003.
“Vpeljava v zgodovino.” *Učiteljski tovariš* 12 (1872): 274–279, 289–294.
Vujisić Živković, N. *Vojislav Bakić i razvoj pedagoške nauke u Srbiji*. Belgrade, Serbia: Univerzitet u Beogradu, Filozofski fakultet, 2012.
Wesendonck, H. *Die Schule Herbart-Ziller und ihre Jünger vor dem Forum der Kritik. Beitrage zur Geschichte, Entwicklung und Kampfweise der neuesten Richtung in der Pädagogik und zum Streite zwischen Dittes und Zillerianern*. Vienna and Leipzig: Verlag von A. Pichler's Witwe & Sohn, 1885.
Zajakin, O. *Die Herbart-Rezeption in der russischen Pädagogik seit der Mitte des 19. Jahrhunderts. Ein Beitrag zur Geschichte des Herbartianismus*. Berlin et al.: Lit Verlag, 2004.
Ziller, T. “Das Leipziger Seminarbuch.” In *Jahrbuch des Vereins für wissenschaftliche Pädagogik*, ed. T. Ziller. Leipzig: In Commision beim Verlag für erziehenden Unterricht, 1874, 99–274.
Ziller, T. *Grundlegung zur Lehre vom erziehenden Unterricht*. Ed. T. Vogt. Leipzig: Verlag von Veit & Comp, 1884. 1st ed. published 1864.
Ziller, T. “Ordnung des akademisch-pädagogischen Seminars.” In *Didaktik in der Unterrichtspraxis*, ed. B. Adl-Amini, J. Oelkers, and D. Neumann, 144–155. Bern und Stuttgart: Haupt, 1979. 1st ed. published 1864.
Ziller, T. *Allgemeine Pädagogik. Dritte Auflage der Vorlesungen über allgemeine Pädagogik*. Ed. K. Just. Leipzig: Verlag von Heinrich Mathes, 1892.
“Zu den Herbart-Ziller-Stoy'schen didaktischen Grundsätzen.” *Laibacher Schulzeitung* 12 (1884): 45–46.
Žlebnik, L. *Obča zgodovina pedagogike*. Ljubljana: Državna založba Slovenije, 1978.

**Erziehung in Wissenschaft und Praxis**

Herausgegeben von Johanna Hopfner



www.peterlang.com